John Vince

Essential Computer Animation fast

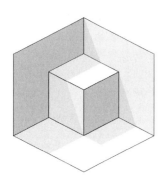

**How to Understand the
Techniques and Potential
of Computer Animation**

 Springer

John Vince, MTech, PhD, FBCS, CEng
School of Media Arts and Communication, Talbot Campus,
Fern Barrow, Poole BH12 5BB, UK

Series Editor
John Cowell, BSc (Hons), MPhil, PhD
Department of Computer and Information Sciences,
De Montfort University, Kents Hill Campus, Hammerwood Gate,
Kents Hill, Milton Keynes MK7 6HP, UK

ISBN 1-85233-141-0 Springer-Verlag London Berlin Heidelberg

British Library Cataloguing in Publication Data
Vince, John 1941-
  Essential computer animation fast : how to understand the
  Techniques and potential of computer animation. –
  (Essential series)
  1. Computer animation   2. Computer graphics
  I. Title   II. Computer animation fast
  006.6'96
ISBN 1852331410

Library of Congress Cataloging-in-Publication Data
Vince, John (John A.)
    Essential computer animation fast / John Vince.
      p. cm. – (Essential series)
      Includes bibliographical references.
      ISBN 1-85233-141-0 (alk. paper)
      1. Computer animation.   I. Title.   II. Essential series (Springer-Verlag)
    TR897.7 V56 1999
    006.6'96—dc21   99-050391

© Springer-Verlag London Limited 2000
Printed in Great Britain

Typesetting: Camera-ready by author
Printed and bound at The Cromwell Press, Trowbridge, Wiltshire
34/3830-543210 Printed on acid-free paper SPIN 10707824

Dedication

to Megan

Acknowledgments

Writing books is relatively easy. A blank sheet of paper is covered quickly with words without too much effort, but a hurdle for any author, especially with a subject like computer animation, is the images. Fortunately, I am lucky working at the National Center for Computer Animation, as I have access to some of the most talented students studying computer animation. One such student is James Hans, who is on a three-year BA in Computer Visualization and Animation. As James seems to spend every waking moment of his life modeling and animating, he was an ideal source of images for this book. As you will discover when you browse through the following chapters, James' pictures have been used to good effect to illustrate what words fail to express. Thank you James for your contribution to this book, especially for the cover and poster design.

I would also like to thank Neil Glasbey, Nigel Sumner, Chris Tucker and the other postgraduate students who allowed me to use their images.

Viewpoint DataLabs, Inc. provided me with some excellent illustrations in Chapter 3 of an elephant, a tree and a human heart.

Finally, I would like to thank Digital-X and Next Limit for providing me with valuable text and images.

Contents

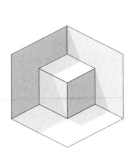

1
What is Computer Animation?

Introduction

Although computers play a vital and important role in applications such as stock control, payroll, billing, invoicing, banking, etc., it is difficult to get too enthusiastic about such applications. On the other hand, when computers are used to create and manipulate images — especially 3D images — one discovers new and exciting worlds that immediately fire the imagination. Such a view may seem rather biased, but having spent nearly all of my working life in computer graphics, it is difficult to be very objective about such matters!

Over the past thirty years, or so, computer graphics has evolved into a sophisticated subject area, and created disciplines such as image processing, digital graphic design, computer games, virtual reality, visualization, medical imaging, multimedia, and last, but not least, computer animation. All of these topics have become major areas of specialization requiring disparate specialist skills. Fortunately, though, there are many common strands of knowledge that make it relatively easy to understand all of these topics without too much effort. However, in spite of the temptation to explore the broader subject of computer graphics, I will restrict myself to the topic of computer animation.

What is computer animation?

This may seem a trivial question to ask, but one I think worth asking. To begin with, traditional animation is concerned with a process of hand-drawing a sequence of images on sheets of celluloid (cel), which are back-painted, individually photographed, and played back on a film projector at 24 frames/second. Perhaps Disney is the name that springs to mind when talking of such animated cartoons.

In the early days of computer graphics, computer programs were developed to mimic this traditional cartoon process. A computer would be used to draw a sequence of line drawings, using some mathematical technique, direct onto paper or cel. Then, after the images were photographed and played back through a projector, an animated effect was obtained. The nature of the animation depended on what had been input into the computer. For example, if two different line drawings had been input it was possible to transform the first image into the second over a period of time. On the other hand, a computer program could have been used to take a mathematical curve such as a spiral and unwind it into a circle. This would have been a difficult task for a cartoon animator, especially if a high degree of precision was required, but it is a trivial exercise for a computer.

Today, computer systems are widely used throughout the cartoon industry and play an important role in automating the tasks of inputting artwork, cleaning up inconsistent line quality, image coloring, image compositing, and special effects such as out-of-focus depth of field. The final animation, however, is still in the form of the traditional cartoon.

Another type of computer animation system has also evolved — one where a computer is used to simulate imaginary 3D worlds, inhabited by objects and creatures that can be animated to move with scary realism. These systems have become so effective that they are regularly used to create special effects in most major movies. *Toy Story* was the first feature film to be made entirely by computer technology, but it has been followed quickly by *A Bug's Life* and *Antz*. This is what is generally understood to mean 3D computer animation, and the interpretation used in this book.

In general, computer animation is concerned with the animation of 3D virtual worlds, but there is nothing to stop one from working in 2D or something in between. The process involves the computer modeling of characters and the sets they inhabit, the motion characteristics used to animate the characters, decorative colors and textures, lighting, and the position and movement of the virtual movie camera. It all seems straightforward, but it is only possible with the help of geometry, mathematics, optics, physics and the natural sciences.

In the early days of computer animation there was no choice but to master these disciplines, and develop bespoke animation software using a computer language such as Fortran. Today, things are very different. Animators now have access to powerful software products such as Sumatra, Maya, 3D Studio MAX, Lightwave and Houdini. Figure 1.1 shows a screen shot of the Softimage animation system.

Although these systems employ extensive mathematical and geometric techniques to create their images, they are hidden from the user. The user's sole task is to translate some creative idea into animation using the features made available through a high-level graphical user interface (GUI). In many instances, very sophisticated effects are initiated by selecting options from pull-down menus. However, before using such an animation system, it is helpful to understand some basic principles that will accelerate the learning process. Such principles are the subject of this book.

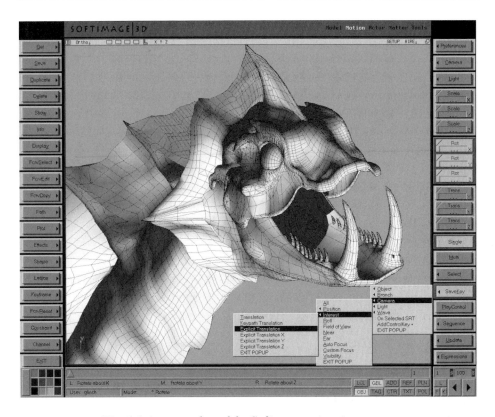

Fig. 1.1 *A screen shot of the Softimage animation system.*

Who should read this book?

If you have suddenly decided to explore the subject of computer animation, then this book will provide a perfect introductory text. Terms and processes are explained in easy-to-understand language, without any mathematical notation. If, at a later date, you need to learn more about the geometric and mathematical techniques that make everything happen, then there are plenty of books that address such matters and are listed in the bibliography.

If, on the other hand, you are just interested in knowing how computers are able to produce animation, then this book will reveal the process, without swamping you with irrelevant detail.

The aims and objectives of this book

The aim of this book is to give the reader a broad knowledge of computer animation without introducing any mathematical notation. After reading the book, the reader should have a clear understanding of the terminology and processes used in computer animation, and should be able to read more advanced texts with confidence. It is particularly suited to someone thinking about buying some computer animation software, and who wants some understanding of the basic jargon and concepts before tackling the system's user manual. The book will also provide a useful reference document when working with some of the commercial computer animation systems.

The book will not endow you with magical skills that will enable you to create wonderful computer animation overnight. This will take time — a lot of time — unless you already have traditional animation skills.

Assumptions made in this book

I have not made very many assumptions about you, the reader. Basically, I assume that you understand what a computer is and how it works. You probably already know that computers can be used to create images. Perhaps you have already seen such images in recent films such as *Titanic, A Bug's Life, The Matrix* and *Antz*, which contain some amazing computer animation. And there is no need to make any assumptions about your knowledge of mathematics, because no mathematical notation is used.

How to use the book

The book has been designed to be read from cover to cover. Each chapter covers concepts and techniques that are developed in subsequent chapters. But obviously where you feel that you are already familiar with the subject of a chapter, then simply jump ahead.

Appendix A includes useful Web sites that you should investigate. Many of the sites contain advice on all aspects of computer animation. There are discussion groups where animators discuss how to achieve an effect in a specific animation system. Not all of it will make sense until you are familiar with the general principles of computer animation, but once you have mastered these, the Web will become a major source of information.

I have also provided Web addresses of companies working in computer animation. Alas it is not a complete list, but hopefully the list is sufficient to enable you to get started and surf the Net on your own.

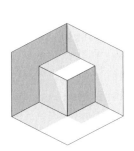

2
Computer Animation

Introduction

In this chapter we take a brief look at the evolution of computer software, and trace its progress to off-the-shelf computer animation software. We also explore how the human visual system can be fooled into converting a sequence of still images into a continuous animation. And finally, we preview the basic features of a computer animation system (CAS).

Animation and computers

We all know that computers are electronic machines that manipulate binary codes to solve problems. We often refer to the binary code as consisting of 'zeros' and 'ones', but at no time will you ever find a 0 or a 1 inside a computer. What you will find are two electronic states 'off' and 'on', which are represented by 0 and 1 for linguistic convenience. Binary code is used to encode all sorts of information in computers. For example, there are unique codes for the digits '0' to '9', lower-case letters 'a' to 'z', upper-case letters 'A' to 'Z', as well as special symbols such as !"£$%^&*()_+=-:;@'~#<,>.?/, etc.

All computers possess hardware circuits that enable them to add, subtract, multiply, divide and compare sequences of binary codes, and these circuits can be activated by a sequence of instructions in the form of a program. In the early days of computers, programming was a painstaking process, and required a programmer to organize a long sequence of binary instructions to solve trivial problems.

It soon became obvious that little progress would be made if programming was restricted to binary instructions, and the idea of a *problem-oriented language* emerged. A problem-oriented language was designed for the convenience of humans, rather than computers. For example, the word 'ADD' was used instead of the code for binary addition, which might have been '00110001'. Similar codes existed for subtract (SUB), multiply (MLT), and divide (DIV). However, the computer could not respond directly to the mnemonics ADD, SUB, MLT and DIV as its language was binary. So, to bridge the gap between the two languages (problem-oriented and binary) a translator program was written to convert the convenient notation of the problem-oriented language into binary. Thus, whenever the translator program read in the code 'ADD' it converted it into '00110001', for example, with similar substitutions for the other codes. Computer programming, then, consisted of three steps: writing a program in a problem-oriented language, translating it into binary, and then running the binary program. If the binary program did not work properly, the programmer returned to the original script, corrected the mistake, and retranslated it into binary. This was a very powerful idea, as computers were used to help us program them.

Translator programs are still used today. For simple languages, such as the one described above, where there is a one-to-one relationship between the two languages, the translator is called an *assembler*. For more high-level languages, such as Fortran, Cobol, C and C++, the name *compiler* is used.

As you may have realized, anyone can invent a new computer language, however, a translator or compiler is required to convert the program script into binary. And writing a compiler is not a trivial task. In recent years, new languages such as VISUAL BASIC, Java and VRML have appeared, and the major computer companies have provided software products to make the appropriate translations to binary.

If programming languages can be invented, is it possible to invent one to do computer animation? Well, the answer is yes. We could invent a language where we could write statements such as DRAW A RED SPHERE 2 UNITS DIAMETER. We would also have to say where the sphere was to be drawn and the camera's position in space recording the scene. But before the computer could process such a command, it would have to be translated into binary. This means that binary code must be available to execute the 'DRAW' command, and the computer must also know what 'RED' means, and the meaning of 'SPHERE 2 UNITS DIAMETER'.

Early computer animation systems were like the one described above, where high-level scripts were written in Fortran or some other language, translated into binary and executed. Whenever a change was made to the animation, the script was modified and translated again. Obviously, this wasted a lot of time, and eventually they were replaced by more efficient systems.

My own system, PICASO, worked along these lines. It was possible to program a computer with a few statements that resulted in some useful images and animation. The following script illustrates the idea:

> *CALL START*
> *CALL FRAME(0.0, 7.0, 0.0, 5.0)*
> *CALL ORIGIN(3.5, 2.5)*
> *CALL EYE(15.0, 15.0, 15.0, 0.0, 0.0, 0.0)*
> *CALL SPHERE(A, 2.0)*
> *CALL DRAWIT(A)*
> *CALL FINISH*
> *END*

Perhaps the most interesting lines in the program are CALL SPHERE and CALL DRAWIT. The CALL SPHERE statement provides the user with the 3D coordinates of a 2" radius sphere, called 'A', and the CALL DRAWIT statement draws a perspective view of the sphere, from the position expressed in the CALL EYE statement. In retrospect, this was a tedious way of animating, but there was no alternative.

Today, a CAS employs an advanced graphical user interface (GUI) to communicate commands. For example, a sphere could be accessed from an internal library of objects using a pull-down menu. It could then be scaled to 2 units diameter, colored red, and positioned anywhere in space, just by using a mouse. No programming is necessary. However, such an approach is only possible with fast computers that support real-time interaction.

A modern CAS is written in a programming language such as C or C++. It is extremely large and consists of millions of instructions. And because of the high commercial value associated with such programs, the original C or C++ script is never released to customers — only the binary version, which runs on a specific type of computer, is made available. The problem with releasing such valuable code is protecting it from being copied by unscrupulous people and sold on the counterfeit market.

As one might expect, it is impossible to design a CAS that can undertake everything an animator will ever require. Therefore, any system will have limitations, and even contain many programming errors that prevent certain features from functioning correctly. Consequently, it is normal for a CAS to be updated once or twice a year to improve its functionality.

Even though a GUI provides an excellent interface for creating animation, there are still many instances where programming is the best solution. Therefore, some systems will provide the user with a scripting facility to complement the GUI. Such scripts, though, are an integral feature of the system, and do not have to be translated into binary. They are 'interpreted' into actions understood by the system directly.

This is probably as far as we need to go at this stage in understanding the features of a CAS. In later chapters we will see how various animation features are executed, and list the properties of specific commercial systems.

The history of animation

Animation has been around in one form or another for over 150 years; some of the important landmarks are listed below:

1824 Peter Roget presented his paper *The persistence of vision with regard to moving objects* to the British Royal Society.

1831 Dr. Joseph Antoine Plateau and Dr. Simon Ritter constructed a machine called a *phenakistoscope*, which produced an illusion of movement by allowing a viewer to gaze at a rotating disk containing small windows, behind which, was another disk containing a sequence of images. When the disks rotated at the correct speed, the synchronization of the windows with the images created an animated effect.

1834 Horner developed the *zoetrope* from Plateau's phenakistoscope.

1872 Eadweard Muybridge began photographing human and animal motion.

1887 Thomas Edison started investigating motion pictures.

1889 Thomas Edison announced his *kinetoscope* which projected a 50 ft length of film in approximately 13 seconds.

1889 George Eastman began the manufacture of photographic film strips using a nitro-cellulose base.

1895 Louis and Auguste Lumière issued a patent for a device called a *cinematograph* capable of projecting moving images.

1896 Thomas Armat designed the *vitascope* which projected the films of Thomas Edison. This machine had a major influence on all subsequent projectors.

1906 J. Stuart Blackton made the first animated film called *Humorous phases of funny faces*.

1908 Emile Cohl produced a film depicting white figures on a black background.

1908 Winsor McCay produced animation using his comic strip character *Little Nemo*.

1909 Winsor McCay produced a cartoon called *Gertie the trained Dinosaur* consisting of 10000 drawings.

1913 Pat Sullivan created an American cartoon series called *Felix the Cat*. J.R. Bray devised *Colonel Heeza Liar* and Sidney Smith created *Old Doc Yak*.

1915 Earl Hurd developed cel animation.

1917 The International Feature Syndicate released many titles including *Silk hat Harry*, *Bringing up Father*, and *Krazy Kat*.

1923 Walt Disney extended Max Fleischer's technique of combining live action with cartoon characters in the film *Alice's Wonderland*.

1926 Lotte Reiniger produced the first feature-length animated film called *Prince Achmed*.

1927 Warner Brothers released *The Jazz Singer* which introduced combined sound and images.

1928 Walt Disney created the first cartoon with synchronized sound called *Mickey Mouse*.

1943 John and James Whitney produced *Five Abstract Film Exercises*.

1945 Harry Smith produced animation by drawing direct onto film.

1957 John Whitney used 17 Bodine motors, 8 Selsyns, 9 differential gear units and 5 ball integrators to create analog computer graphics.

1961 John Whitney used differential gear mechanisms to create film and television title sequences.

1964 Ken Knowlton, working at Bell Laboratories, started developing computer techniques for producing animated movies.

Animation and the human visual system

Persistence of vision

The process of seeing begins when light enters our eyes and stimulates the light-sensitive rod and cone photoreceptors in the retinas. Electrical signals are then transported via the optic nerve to the brain where the sensation of an image is experienced. Because a chemical process is used to convert the light energy into electrical energy, the conversion is not instantaneous — but takes approximately 25 ms. When the photoreceptors are excited they require a little time to relax to their original state. It is this chemical latency that accounts for the blurring of fast, moving objects, and is called persistence of vision.

Another feature of the visual system is known as the *phi phenomenon*. This is the effect we observe when one light source is switched off, and another light, close by, is immediately switched on. Providing that the lights are spatially and temporally close to one another, we observe a single light moving from the first position to the second, rather than two distinct events. Gregory (1986) argues that this is not the brain filling in the gap with an electrical charge, as proposed by Gestalt psychologists, but the activation of the retinal movement system.

Fusion frequency

Persistence of vision and the phi phenomenon (whatever its mechanism) are vital to the action of cinema and television, as it means that the human visual system can be fooled into believing that a sequence of still images is actually continuous. In fact, there is a minimum rate at which a flickering light source must be repeated before it appears continuous. This is known as the *fusion frequency* and is dependent on the brightness of the light source. The brighter the light the higher the fusion frequency. Cine-projectors, for example, project images at 24 frames/second, and each frame is interrupted three times by a rotating blade to increase the flicker rate to 72 images/second. In television an image frame is divided into two fields containing the odd and even horizontal lines, which are repeated alternately. The UK's PAL system displays each frame 25 times/second (Hz) giving a total field rate of 50 Hz, whereas the USA's NTSC system displays each frame at 30 Hz giving a total field rate of 60 Hz.

Computer animation works by producing 25 or 30 frames for each second of video, or 24 frames of film. Thus, for a 10-second animated film 240 (10×24) images are required, and for a 90 minute feature film 129,600 (90×60×24) frames are needed. What is more, if each frame takes 20 minutes to produce, the entire film will take a single computer 1800 days to produce! Which is why hundreds of computers are required for such projects.

Because processing power is so important to the production of commercial films, many companies rely upon supercomputers to undertake their rendering. Another approach is to distribute the rendering task over a large number of smaller processors. Such a system is called a *render farm*.

Computer animation

Apart from thinking up a story, which is probably the hardest task, there are seven processes in computer animation: modeling, decoration, animating, lighting, camera control, rendering and compositing.

Modeling

Modeling is concerned with the construction of the virtual characters, objects and sets used in a story. It presents real problems for an animator, as decisions have to be taken about a modeling strategy where objects have to look real, can be animated, decorated and textured, and can be rendered in the form of an image as fast as possible. It is relatively easy to build complex models that contain several hundred thousand polygons. But in the computer games industry, great importance is placed upon the skill of modeling characters using the smallest number of surface elements. Every surplus polygon has to be animated and rendered, which takes up valuable game time, and ultimately degrades the speed of the game.

Models may appear at different distances in a scene, and it is often necessary to construct two or three versions of a model with appropriate levels of detail. As the model recedes into the distance, substitutions are made with models of lower levels of detail. Great care is needed to hide these transitions, but subtle scene cutting is an effective solution to this problem.

Modeling solid objects such as furniture, cars, buildings, etc. is relatively straightforward. However, flexible objects such as hands, faces, animals, plants, etc. require careful attention. The main problem with such objects is finding a modeling strategy that copes with the joins and joints between different features. For example, in facial animation, when the mouth opens wide the skin tissue forming the cheeks moves over the skull to take up a new position. If this level of realism is required, considerable effort is necessary to control this behavior. See the excellent modeling by Chris Tucker in plates 1 to 4.

Apart from solid and flexible models, we need to model hair, water, rain, snow, smoke, mist, etc. Some can be modeled from polygons, but other techniques have been developed and will be examined later.

Decoration

Having modeled the geometric skin of an object, the next stage is to decorate it with color and texture. An object can be painted any color, simply by assigning an appropriate mix of the primary colors, red, green and blue. These color values are stored alongside the object's geometric data, and are accessed whenever the object is rendered. Even a single polygon can be assigned a specific color, it is just a question of isolating the polygon and assigning a color.

Surface detail can be in the form of an image, texture or bumps, and is achieved by scanning into the computer appropriate images, which are projected onto the surface when the object is rendered. If the object moves, or the camera moves relative to the object, the renderer automatically adjusts the texture for perspective. Professional computer animation systems provide the animator with a library of textures that include wood grain, concrete, metallic finishes, clouds, animal skin, etc., but as one might expect, facilities must exist to scan in an image, or create one using a digital paint system.

Objects can also be assigned various material properties such as roughness and shininess, and even effects such as translucency and transparency. These parameters are input via the GUI, and when the object is rendered are used to create the appropriate effect.

Animating

This is the most crucial stage and reveals the user's ability to bring an object to life. And no matter how many tools a CAS may provide, if the user is not aware of how things move the resulting animation will be sterile. Human motion, for example, is very complex. The way we walk, sit, run, jump, laugh, wave, fall, swim, etc. are so ingrained in our memory, the smallest error jars the eye. Fortunately, it is not always necessary to mimic such behavior with great realism, but when that is the objective, the human visual system is very unforgiving.

The format of traditional animation is the cartoon. And although cartoons can arouse all sorts of emotions, we always know that the images are drawings. On the other hand, the world of computer animation can be anything from flat cartoon characters to 3D scenes that are indistinguishable from the real thing. Thus when images are rendered with great realism, there is a natural expectation for the animation to be equally realistic. This is a complex subject that deserves a deeper and wider discussion and cannot be addressed here. Nevertheless, one cannot underestimate the skills of observation required by computer animators.

A CAS provides a variety of tools to simplify the task of animating objects, and must include techniques such as key-framing, scripting, inverse kinematics and physical simulation. These will all be described in detail in Chapter 4. But whatever tool is used, the real advantage of using a computer is its ability to playback the animation during the design stage. The animator makes the first attempt at animating a scene, and instructs the CAS to playback the animation. The images may be in the form of lines, rather than full color, as there are few computers that can render complex scenes in real time (25 to 30 Hz), however, there is sufficient information to assess the movement of characters. When necessary, the CAS can be instructed to render the animation, store the images on disk, and play these back in real time.

Animators will spend many days, weeks, months, or even years bringing to life the visual ideas expressed in storyboard form. The success of the result, however, has little to do with which CAS was used. It hinges entirely upon the original storyboard, and how adept the animator was in interpreting the story.

Lighting

At this stage of the process we have a collection of virtual models and sets, that have been decorated and can be animated. The next stage is to light the scene with virtual lights.

In the early days of computer graphics, the simplest method of creating a colored image was to use the primary colors assigned to a polygon or object. The result was fast, but very bland. The next step was to introduce a virtual light source whose color, intensity and position determined the quality of light reflected by an object. If the virtual light was switched off, then nothing was seen. The idea of an ambient light level ensured that when all light sources were switched off, there was always a contribution of background light that remained constant.

A CAS provides facilities to position any number of light sources in space. The light sources may radiate light in all directions, in one particular direction, or in the form of a spotlight. The light may be white, colored, flashing, flickering, stationary, moving, a point source, or an area source, such as the Sun.

With such an array of lights, one might expect that it is easy to light a scene and create realistic images — but this is not so. For when we look at the real world, we are reacting to light that has originated from the Sun and artificial lights, reflected off walls, ceilings, curtains, and a thousand and one other surfaces before it enters our eyes. The resulting image includes soft shadows, delicate color changes across a surface, color bleeding, complex reflections, etc. This level of realism cannot be obtained simply by positioning a few virtual light sources; it requires the computer to simulate the physical behavior of light at a virtual level. This can be achieved by using the techniques of ray tracing and radiosity, which are explained later.

Camera control

By camera control, I mean the various parameters and techniques that can be assigned to the virtual movie camera recording the animation. In fact, the paradigm of emulating a real movie camera is used only to specify the point in space from where the animation is observed, and the optical characteristics of the virtual lens.

Basically, the camera can be positioned anywhere in space, even inside an object! It requires three angles to control its angular orientation and a focal length for its lens. As these parameters are numerical quantities, the CAS can easily modify them to emulate the physical characteristics of a real camera.

A camera can be moved dynamically in space to track an activity, or even flown along a complex 3D path during a specific sequence of frames. The GUI provides very efficient tools for refining such moves, and enables the camera to accelerate away from an initial position and decelerate towards a new location.

A CAS can also simulate lens flares, which arise when light reflects between the optical elements of a compound lens. These artifacts are generally introduced into computer-animated sequences to fool the viewer into believing that the images are not computer-generated. Figure 2.1 shows the GUI used by 3D Studio MAX for introducing a lens flare. The animator can control properties such as the number of flare 'spikes', radial transparency, size angle, hue, etc.

Rendering

The rendering stage is where the data describing the geometry, surface properties, and lighting information are translated into an image. The time required to achieve this depends upon the complexity of the scene, the resolution and quality of the image, and ultimately the speed of the computer. In general, this varies between a few seconds to several minutes, but some computers can render in real time with a 30 Hz update rate, and are used in flight simulation and virtual reality applications.

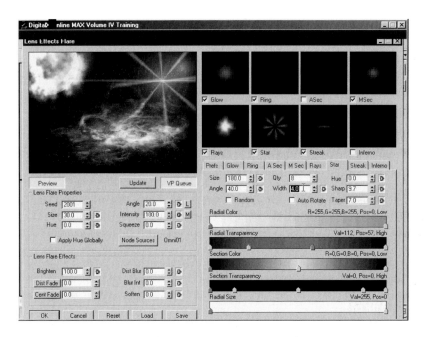

Fig. 2.1 *The GUI used by 3D Studio MAX to insert a lens flare.*
(Image courtesy DigitalX)

The final image is written to disk as a file of pixel data containing the levels of red, green and blue. When all the frames have been rendered, the CAS can play the images back on the user's screen, before transferring them to film or video.

The renderer needs to know the aspect ratio and resolution of the image. The aspect ratio encodes the height and width of the image, whilst the resolution controls the number of horizontal scan lines. For video the aspect ratio is 3:4 or 16:9 and the resolution is approximately 500 lines, depending on whether the UK's PAL or the USA's NTSC system is being used. Armed with this information, the renderer computes the levels of red, green and blue for each pixel in the image.

The design of renderers has advanced considerably over recent years, and today we tend to take for granted the high-quality images they produce. However, renderers are not identical programs — they all seem to leave their 'fingerprints' behind, and some animators easily recognize which CAS was used to create an animation.

Because the rendering process entails so many ideas, I will curtail this overview at this point, and return to a detailed explanation in Chapter 3.

Compositing

The early pioneers of film did not have access to computers or the electronic technology used in television. Consequently, any special effects had to be filmed on the set. The idea of filming actors against a back-projection screen enabled an incredible range of effects to be created without endangering life, or incurring the cost of filming outside the studio. Today, this original idea has evolved into blue or green screen systems that enable one image source to be composited with another. This process is also used widely in computer animation, where one visual element can be composited with another, without leaving any artifacts that betray its origin. Plate 5 shows someone photographed against a blue screen and Plate 6 shows the person integrated into a computer-generated background.

Conclusion

We now have a good idea what computer animation is about. It involves the activities of modeling, decorating, animating, lighting, camera control, rendering and compositing. They are not always as discrete as this, but large projects are often divided into these activities to simplify project management. Furthermore, it is unreasonable to expect a computer animator to excel in all of these areas; hence increasingly one finds job specifications for modelers, artists, animators, envelopers and compositors.

The computer games and the digital special effects industries do not expect their staff to know everything about computer animation. In the computer games sector, people with skills in building realistic characters with the minimum of polygons are highly sought after. In the digital special effects sector, skilled people are needed to light a computer model that has to be composited with live action, or who can take the virtual skeleton of an extinct animal and dress it with realistic muscles.

In the following chapter we explore concepts of computer graphics relevant to computer animation.

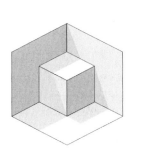

3
3D Computer Graphics

Introduction

Computer graphics is a very broad subject area and supports the disciplines of image processing, visualization, virtual reality, computer-aided design (CAD) and computer animation. In this chapter I will explain the basic concepts of computer graphics so that in the following chapter on computer animation techniques, there will be no need to continuously pause and define individual computer graphics terms.

Having banished mathematical notation from this book I will have to communicate some technical concepts with the aid of words and diagrams. For those who wish to discover more about the mathematical ideas behind the computer algorithms, there are many excellent books waiting to be read.

From computer graphics to computer animation

When computer graphics first started to emerge in the early 1960s, it was difficult to imagine that a day would come when computers would be creating 3D color images in real time. To begin with, computers were so large and expensive it did not enter anyone's head that one day we would have portable computers capable of playing back animation with stereophonic sound. However, after 40 years of technological invention such machines do exist, and who knows what will exist in another 40 years.

Early display devices consisted of graph plotters, storage tubes, video displays and frame-stores. To a certain extent they all still exist, albeit exploiting different technologies. Graph plotters are still in use, but laser and bubble-jet printers have cornered the market of high-quality printing. Storage tubes have disappeared and been replaced by high-resolution raster displays, which made possible the implementation of graphical user interfaces.

A frame-store is a memory device for storing a single image, and when the first one appeared it was a large cabinet storing 0.5 MB of RAM. This was an incredible amount of memory compared to the host main computer, which only possessed 32 KB! Today, there is no need for such a store — an image can be rendered using software and stored in a computer's local RAM, and then written to hard disk. However, when one needs to render animation quickly, a computer graphics board with integral memory is an essential component. In this mode the renderer generates code that instructs the graphics board to create an image. The image quality will not be as high as the software renderer, but is much faster, and speeds up the animation design process.

Whilst these developments in hardware were taking place, computer languages were improving, together with interactive software tools. In the 1980s computer animation systems appeared and have evolved into today's systems.

In parallel with these developments in hardware and software, researchers were solving all sorts of computer graphic problems. These ranged from how to draw a straight line on a pixel screen, to simulating soft shadows using radiosity. It is these techniques that we will explore.

To begin with, I will start with some basic principles of computer graphics and continue with modeling strategies, lighting, rendering and special effects.

Principles of computer graphics

We already know that the internal world of a computer is organized as binary code, therefore we must create some more convenient world if we are to make any headway in creating 3D images. Rather than invent some totally new notation, we use various branches of mathematics that have been around for thousands of years. In particular the work of Euclid and Pythagoras is very relevant, as they laid the foundations for the geometric problems we encounter in computer graphics. Euclid's work on triangles help us compute perspective views of virtual objects and the theorem of Pythagoras pops up in virtually every computer graphics technique.

Let us take a look at the tools we use to construct a virtual 3D world in software. We begin with Cartesian coordinates.

Cartesian coordinates

One of the central principles of computer graphics is the use of Cartesian coordinates to locate a point in space. Figure 3.1 shows a set of 3D Cartesian axes (90° to each other) labeled X, Y, and Z, intersecting at the origin. The position of the point P is uniquely identified by the three measurements x, y, and z, which are called the coordinates of P. Typically, these coordinates are enclosed in brackets (x, y, z), and are always defined in this alphabetic sequence. This triplet of numbers is a unique definition of the point P.

The point *P*, or any other point, can be used to locate the position of a camera, light source, or a specific point on an object. What is important to realize is that inside a computer, three numbers represent a point in space. Furthermore, once we have access to some numeric quantity, it can be altered within a computer program.

It is worth noting that the coordinate system showed in figure 3.1 is a *right-handed coordinate* system. This means that when using your right hand, you can align your thumb with the X-axis, your index finger with the Y-axis, and your middle finger with the Z-axis. If you attempt to use your left hand, you will discover that the Z-axis points in the opposite direction. Commercial animation systems use both conventions; not only that, some choose the Z-axis as the vertical axis. So you should pay special attention to these conventions when working with an animation system.

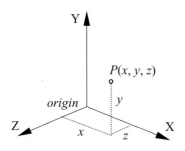

Fig. 3.1 *A set of Cartesian axes.*

Modeling simple objects

Many objects in the real world such as tables, cupboards, desks, boxes, etc. are constructed from flat surfaces, where each surface is defined by a series of edges, and each edge is associated with two corners. In the world of computer graphics, geometric shapes called *polygons*, with 3, 4, 5 or more edges represent such surfaces. But instead of corners, we use the word *vertices*. Figure 3.2 shows a triangular polygon with vertices P_1, P_2 and P_3. As each vertex has three coordinates, nine numbers represent it. For example, if the coordinates for the vertices are $P_1 = (1, 5, 10)$, $P_2 = (10, 1, 9)$ and $P_3 = (12, 10, 1)$, the triangle could be stored inside a computer as three groups of coordinates, as shown in table 3.1.

Table 3.1 *A triangle is stored inside a computer as a table of coordinates.*

Vertex	X	Y	Z
P_1	1	5	10
P_2	10	1	9
P_3	12	10	1

Even though a polygon has two sides, some computer animation systems may only recognize one of them as visible. For example, the triangle in figure 3.2 could be visible from above, but invisible when looking from below. Another convention applies to the direction of the vertices. For instance, in figure 3.2 the vertex sequence P_1, P_2, P_3 is anti-clockwise when viewed from above, but clockwise when viewed from below. When a polygon is defined it is conventional to be consistent about vertex sequences.

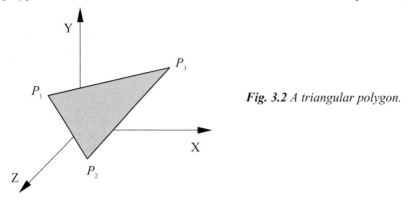

Fig. 3.2 *A triangular polygon.*

The simplest 3D solid object that can be constructed from triangles is the tetrahedron, which has four triangular sides, as shown in figure 3.3. Figure 3.4 shows views of a cube (6 squares), a tetrahedron (4 triangles), an octahedron (8 triangles), a dodecahedron (12 hexagons), and an icosahedron (20 triangles). The mathematician Euler (1707–1783), discovered the following relationship between the edges, faces and vertices of any polyhedron: *Faces + Vertices = Edges + 2*. For example, a cube has 6 faces, 8 vertices and 12 edges and an octahedron has 8 faces, 6 vertices and 12 edges.

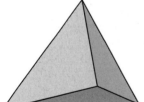

Fig. 3.3 *A tetrahedron constructed from 4 triangles.*

So we can see that it is not too difficult to construct regular geometric objects. Unfortunately, real-world objects are very often irregular. Nevertheless, with the aid of interactive modeling tools it is possible to build a plethora of objects from flat surfaces. Indeed, it is possible to design 3D models simply by specifying the coordinates of the vertices, but it is very easy to introduce errors in the form of twisted surfaces. For example, figure 3.5 shows two views of a cube, the left one with planar (flat) sides, and the right one with twisted sides. Although the twisted cube in figure 3.5 could exist, its surfaces would be curved, and a single planar polygon cannot be used to represent such an object.

Fig. 3.4 *A cube, tetrahedron, octahedron, dodecahedron and icosahedron.*

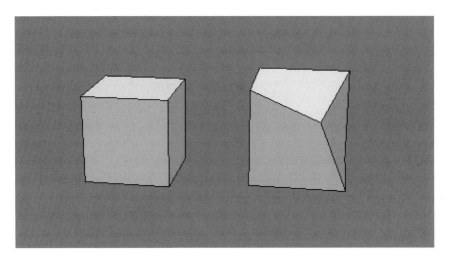

Fig. 3.5 *A cube with flat sides and twisted sides.*

To model really smooth objects such as a sphere or a torus, three techniques are available: the first is to use many small polygons; the second is to use surface patches; and the third is to use mathematical equations. Figure 3.6 shows a sphere and a torus constructed from polygons. The faceted surfaces are very obvious; however we could improve matters by doubling the number of polygons. Although this would improve the appearance, it would double the amount of information stored inside the computer, and also increase the time needed to render the image. In some circumstances, this does not matter, but in computer games, virtual reality and flight simulation, it is essential to keep the number of polygons to a minimum.

Surface patches employ mathematical techniques for representing a small portion of a smooth surface, which can be joined together to form very complex surfaces such as a face or a car body. The ideas behind Bézier and NURBS patches are described later in this chapter.

Certain objects such as a sphere, a cone, a torus, a cylinder, and an ellipsoid, can be represented by mathematical equations. These can be used to form more complex structures and are used by a computer-aided design strategy called *constructive solid geometry* (CSG). Although this is a very important area of computer graphics, it is not widely used within the computer animation sector.

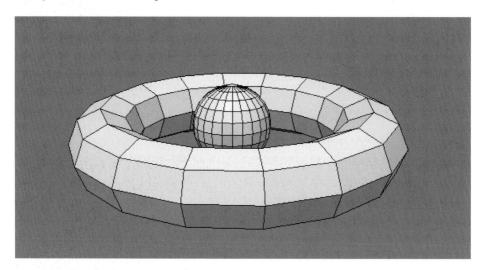

Fig. 3.6 A sphere and a torus constructed from planar polygons.

Interactive modeling

Nichimen's *Nendo* system is an excellent tool for demonstrating just how effective an interactive modeler can be. For example, figure 3.7 shows how moving an individual vertex, edge or polygon can modify the geometry of a torus. To begin with a torus is copied from Nendo's internal library. Then simply by clicking on the required element using a mouse, it is possible to interactively create a new object. When an edge or vertex is moved, the number of polygons remains the same; however, when a polygon is moved, the modeler automatically introduces the extra polygons to maintain the geometric integrity of the surface.

Figure 3.8 shows how holes are created in a cube. We begin with a cube taken from Nendo's internal library. Two opposite sides are identified and the *Inset* feature is selected. This 'shrinks' the polygons forming each side, and replaces each polygon by five new polygons. Then the inner polygons of both sides are identified, and joined using the *Bridge* feature, which creates the final hole. The entire exercise only takes a few seconds.

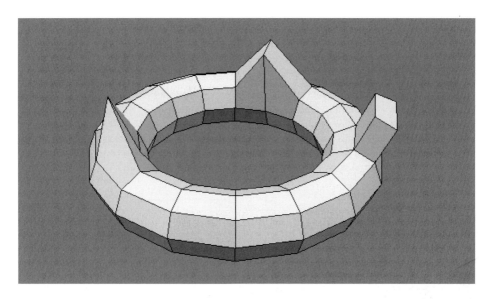

***Fig. 3.7** The surface geometry of a torus has been modified by moving a vertex, an edge and a polygon.*

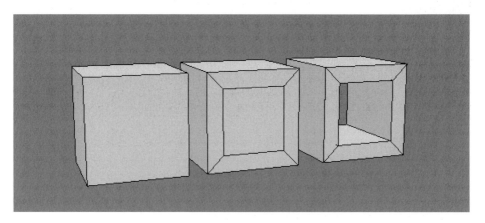

***Fig. 3.8** Three stages to create a cube with a hole using Nendo.*

Modeling assemblies

More complex objects can be built from assemblies of geometric primitives. For example, a table may be modeled from a rectangular top and four identical legs, and a chest of drawers would only require one drawer copied several times, with the associated cabinet. However, there would be no need to model the individual drawers if they were not to be animated. It would be sufficient to model the surface detail to give the impression that the drawers actually existed.

3D libraries

Animation systems generally provide the user with a library of 3D objects, but they may only contain simple geometric primitives. If you require something more esoteric such as a human heart, an elephant, a submarine, or a tree, then it's highly likely that Viewpoint DataLabs can help. They provide a valuable service to the computer animation industry by maintaining and selling a large database of 3D models that can be purchased individually or as collections. For example, figure 3.9 shows a human heart revealing its complex interior. The model is extremely accurate as it is based upon the geometry of a real heart.

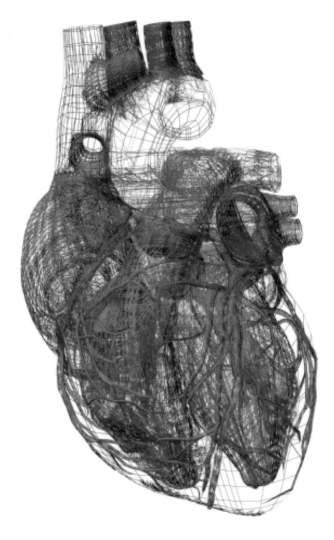

Fig. 3.9 *A polygonal human heart. (Image courtesy Viewpoint DataLabs)*

Figure 3.10 shows the geometry of an elephant, which has probably been digitized from a physical model.

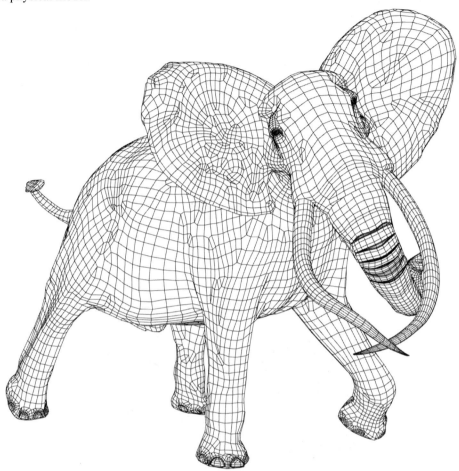

Fig. 3.10 *A polygonal 3D elephant. (Image courtesy Viewpoint DataLabs)*

Finally, figure 3.11 shows a 3D polygonal model of a tree. Such a model could have been digitized by hand, or even grown using a program. The latter technique would have involved providing a program with a set of rules describing the characteristics of the tree. The rules would describe how branches would be formed; how they would be distributed about the trunk; the angle between a major branch and a minor branch; how the branches reduce in size; and how leaves are distributed. If stochastic (random) procedures are introduced into the program, in the form of random numbers, the tree acquires characteristics that give it a life-like quality, rather than looking as though it has been grown to a formula.

Fig. 3.11 *A 3D polygonal tree. (Image courtesy Viewpoint DataLabs)*

Internal representation of geometry

It should now be obvious that faceted objects can be created from a collection of polygons defined by edges and vertices. However, we still require a way to store these numbers inside a computer such that the integrity of the geometry is maintained no matter how it's modified. A *data structure* is used to hold data in a particular order within a computer system, and one such technique is called a *winged-edge* data structure. The name comes from the basic atom of geometry stored within the data structure, and is illustrated in figure 3.12. The figure shows a rectangular box constructed from 6 sides, 12 edges, and 8 vertices. Because each pair of adjacent sides share a common edge, and each edge is defined by two vertices, which belong to other edges dividing other adjacent sides, a simple data structure can be used to link everything together. The data structure is shown in figure 3.12 as a vertical line forming an edge, and wing-like elements on the top and bottom, identify the vertices and their associated edges. Whenever a vertex is moved to a new position, the integrity of the edge geometry remains sound, so too, is the boundary of the polygon. So no matter how vertices, edges and polygons are moved around, the winged-edge data structure will not introduce any holes or gaps.

Remember that the geometry of a polygonal object is stored in the form of vertices represented as three coordinates, and a data structure is used to relate the vertices to edges, and edges to polygons. The winged-edge data structure may not be found in every CAS, but something similar is required.

Unless you are intending to do some serious programming, there is no need to study data structures any further.

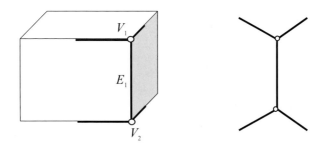

Fig. 3.12 *The box on the left has 6 sides, 12 edges and 8 vertices, linked together using the winged-edge data structure on the right. The edge E_1 is the boundary between two sides and is delimited by the vertices V_1 and V_2.*

Modeling curves

As we have just seen, a wide variety of objects can be modeled from a collection of polygons, and it is obvious that the surface has a polygonal skin. However, if we wish to model objects that have a smooth and continuous surface, we have to employ other strategies. One such technique is called a *surface patch*, and has a mathematical basis. But in spite of its mathematical origin, it is still easy to understand. Let's approach it by first considering the modeling of a 2D curve.

One way to model a curve is to create a chain of very short, straight edges, such that they appear smooth. The drawback with this technique is that it uses many edges and the curve is not really that smooth. Furthermore, it can be very difficult to modify the curve into another shape without introducing kinks. An alternative approach is to employ a mathematical equation.

If you have studied graphs in math classes, you may recall that a straight line is called a *linear equation*. This is because a horizontal displacement along the line has an associated vertical displacement. This feature is called *linear*, and is illustrated in figure 3.13. The ratio of these displacements (Y_1/X_1 and Y_2/X_2) defines the slope of the line and constant, no matter where the measurement is made. Mathematicians call line equations *first degree* equations. (Now I know what you are thinking. I promised that I would not introduce any mathematics, and I haven't. But I have had to introduce some of the jargon, because it has found its way into computer animation systems.)

Curves, on the other hand, have changing slopes. For example, when we throw a stone in the air, it traces out a familiar arc called a parabola, which belongs to the *quadratic* family of curves (called *second degree* equations). Figure 3.14 shows a collection of second degree quadratics. A quadratic's slope cannot be constant, otherwise it would not be curved! A parabola has a very simple mathematical equation, and different shapes are obtained by changing numbers within the equation. However, one has to use algebra to form a particular shape.

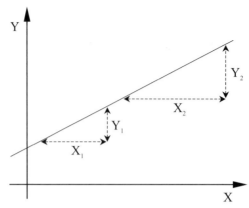

***Fig 3.13** A straight line is described as linear because its slope is constant.*

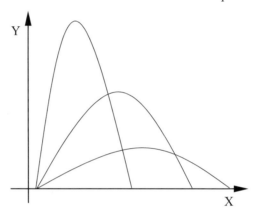

***Fig. 3.14** A family of parabolas.*

Bézier curves

Fortunately for us, there are many ways of forming curves, and Pierre Bézier developed one such technique when working for Renault in France. The technique is very flexible as it only requires the user to fix the end vertices of the curve, and uses a separate *control vertex* (CV) to shape the quadratic curve. Figure 3.15 shows such an arrangement, where A and B are the end points of the curve and C_v is the CV. A special equation is then used to model the line internally within the computer. A useful feature of Bézier curves is that they always exist within the boundary lines connecting A, B and C_v. Another useful feature is that the slopes of the curve at A and B are equal to the slopes of the lines A–C_v and B–C_v respectively. Joining a sequence of them together forms longer curves. Figure 3.16 shows an example where two Bézier segments are used to form a continuous quadratic curve.

In figure 3.16 we see a Bézier curve segment shaped by C_{v1} between A and B, and a second segment is shaped by C_{v2} between B and D. The interesting thing to note is that there is no kink at B where the two segments meet. This is because the curve's slope at B is the slope of the line C_{v1}–B, which is equal to slope of the line B–C_{v2}, so the two curve segments blend into one. Now this is a powerful technique for creating curves: first, there is no explicit equation to manipulate; second, the curve's shape is formed by positioning a control vertex; third, long curves can be formed from shorter segments; and fourth, there is slope continuity at the joins. Perhaps the one disadvantage of Bézier curves is that whenever a control vertex is moved the entire shape of the curve is disturbed.

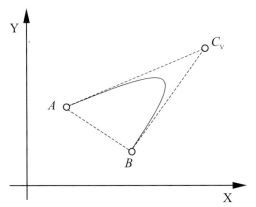

Fig. 3.15 *A second degree Bézier curve formed by three points A, B and C_V.*

Quadratic (second degree) curves only have one bend in their shape, but *cubic* (*third degree*) curves have two, as shown in figure 3.17. These, too, have a Bézier form, as shown in figure 3.18, but this time two CVs are used to shape the curve.

In figure 3.18 we see that a cubic curve has been formed between *A* and *B*, where the control vertex C_{V1} pulls the curve to the right and C_{V2} pulls it to the left. Cubic Bézier curve segments can also be joined together to form even more complex shapes; slope continuity is preserved if we employ the strategy described for the quadratic curve.

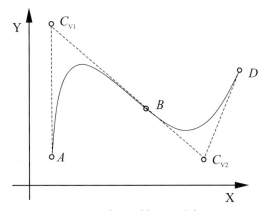

Fig. 3.16 *A second degree curve formed by two Bézier curve segments.*

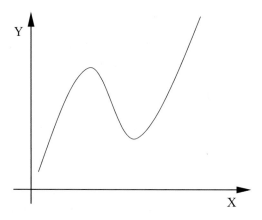

Fig. 3.17 *A cubic curve can have two bends.*

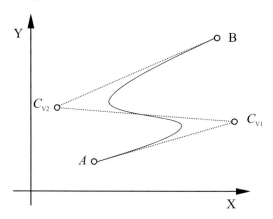

Fig. 3.18 *A cubic Bézier curve shaped by two CVs.*

To summarize:
- Bézier curves offer a convenient way of forming complex curves between two end points using a control vertex, which pushes and pulls the curve into a desired shape.
- The concept of a control vertex is very important in computer animation and is often abbreviated to CV.
- Slope continuity between curve segments can be controlled and prevents any visible kink.
- Bézier curves are typically quadratic (second degree) or cubic (third degree), although higher degree forms are possible.
- Whenever a CV is moved, the entire curve shape is disturbed.
- Bézier curves can be 2D or 3D.

NURBS

Although Bézier curves are very useful, NURBS curves are even more effective and ubiquitous in the world of computer animation. To begin with, I will explain the name NURBS, which is an abbreviation for Non-Uniform Rational B-Spline. The word spline comes from the ship building industry where long, thin pieces of wood called splines are used to shape a ship's hull and have a very simple mathematical description. The letter 'B' comes from C. de Boor, who, like Pierre Bézier (Renault), and Paul De Casteljau (Citroen), was behind the early work in the mathematics of splines.

A rational number such as 3.5 can be represented as the ratio of 7/2, whereas a number like π (3.14159265) or 2 is irrational, as it cannot be represented as a simple ratio. Therefore, a rational B-spline intimates that two equations are used in the form of a ratio, which mathematically is very convenient. The use of 'Non-Uniform' requires a lengthy mathematical explanation, which is beyond the scope of this text, and should not concern the reader.

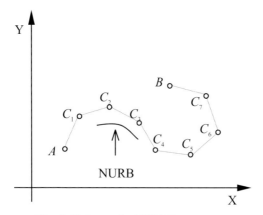

Fig. 3.19 *Part of a NURBS curve.*

Basically, a NURBS curve is similar to a Bézier curve, in that it is formed between two end points, but any number of CVs can be used to shape the curve. Figure 3.19 shows the end points *A* and *B* and seven CVs. It also shows part of the cubic NURBS curve, which has been shaped by local CVs. The entire NURBS curve is developed by taking successive overlapping groups of four CVs between the two end points.

Figure 3.20 illustrates the GUI provided by 3D Studio MAX to create a NURBS curve. The top left-hand window shows the developing NURBS curve with its CVs, whilst the other windows show the front, left and perspective elevations.

A further advantage of NURBS is found in the *weightings* associated with the CVs. Here the modeler can pull the curve closer to the CV by associating a higher numerical weight with the CV, which amplifies its influence.

NURBS is a very powerful technique for developing curves and has the following advantages:

- There is no limit to the number of CVs.

- Curve continuity is preserved between segments of NURBS.
- Moving a CV affects only the local shape of the curve.
- Only the end points and the CVs have to be stored.
- NURBS works in 2D and 3D.
- CVs can be weighted.

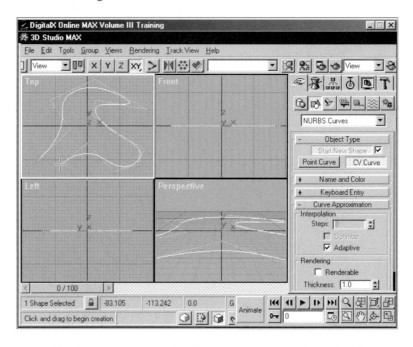

Fig. 3.20 *Creating a NURBS primitive using 3D Studio MAX.*
(Image courtesy DigitalX)

Surface patches

Having discovered how Bézier curves and NURBS are shaped by CVs, we can translate these ideas into a Bézier or NURBS surface patch.

When shaping a curve a CV acts like a magnet by attracting the curve until overpowered by the influence of a neighboring CV. This 'magnetic' action of CVs can also be simulated mathematically to define a surface, as shown in figure 3.21. The figure shows a 3×3 grid of CVs. Four of them (*A*, *B*, *C*, and *D*) form the corners of the patch and the other five CVs shape the surface patch.

The figure also shows the curved edges of the surface patch, which appears to be draped between the four corners. And simply by moving any of the other CVs, the surface can be pushed and pulled into shape. However, because only one CV exists between two corner CVs, the surface patch has a parabolic shape and is called a second degree surface.

If, however, we use a 4×4 grid of CVs, there are two CVs between two corner CVs, which would form a cubic (third degree) surface patch. Figure 3.22 shows such an arrangement and we can see that the edges of the patch have the undulations associated with a cubic curve.

Like Bézier curves, Bézier surface patches can be joined to one another to form a complex surface. And if a pair of adjoining patches share a common edge slope, the join will be free of any kinks.

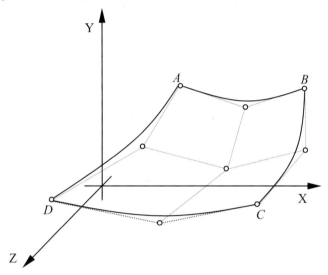

Fig. 3.21 *A quadratic Bézier surface patch formed from 9 CVs.*

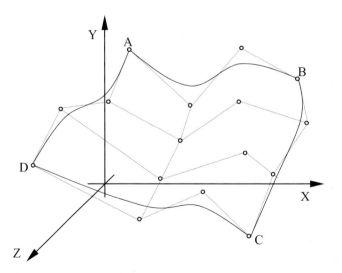

Fig. 3.22 *A cubic Bézier surface patch with 16 CVs.*

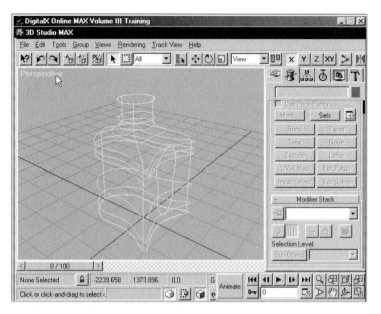

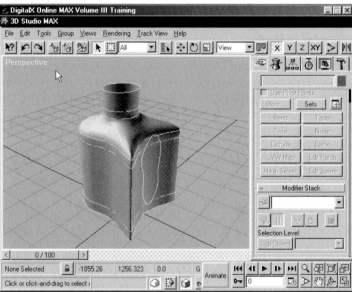

Fig. 3.23 *The top view shows a bottle formed by a family of NURBS, whilst the bottom view shows the rendered surface. (Image courtesy DigitalX)*

Today, modeling with NURBS has become extremely easy. Very powerful GUIs exist that enable a modeler to specify a few closed curves, from which a surface can be constructed. As an illustration, consider the two views shown in figure 3.23. The top view shows a series of cross-sections represented by NURBS, and the bottom view shows the rendered surface. What could be easier!

Now that we have seen how geometric skins can be created from polygons and surface patches, the benefits of surface patches are obvious:

- A cubic surface patch only requires a 4×4 grid of 3D CVs for its definition (i.e. 48 numbers), and can represent a smooth, complex surface.
- Surface patches can be joined together to form complete surfaces.
- Local geometric features can be introduced by manipulating a CV.
- Only the CVs are stored.
- They can be mixed with polygons.
- The CVs can be moved to create animations.

Procedural modeling

So far we have only looked at modeling techniques that involve our direct intervention, but the subject of *procedural modeling* enables us to design automatically certain structures. For example, say we wanted to model a brick wall using individual bricks. Obviously, we could model this manually, but it would be tedious. Instead, a computer procedure (algorithm) could be designed, that given the length and height of the wall, would compute and organize the layout of the bricks automatically. If one thinks about it, the entire process of building the wall could be animated using a procedure. One can imagine a pile of bricks modeled using a procedure and each brick is given a number. Another procedure is designed to 'pick up' one brick at a time, and 'fly' it to its destination. When the first row of bricks is laid, the procedure automatically offsets the second row by half a brick, and continues building the wall without any further intervention. This type of animation is called *procedural animation*, and is discussed in the following chapter.

Another type of procedural modeling uses pseudo-random numbers to control the size of triangles in a mesh. We could start the process by specifying a 'seed' triangle, and then allow a procedure to design the remaining triangles using certain criteria. The vertices of the triangles could have been three-dimensional, which would have created a 3D mesh and be used as an imaginary terrain. One problem with such a technique is that there is no guarantee that one will like the finished result. But one could readily design a procedure that invented hundreds of examples, and then chose the 'best' one. Procedural modeling techniques are used to design trees, texture surfaces, build clouds, add surface clutter, create fractal landscapes, etc.

Laser scanners

Where a physical model exists, it is possible to capture its surface geometry using a laser scanner. Scanners are available that can scan an entire person, down to small hand-held models such as the HLS system from Polhemus. Figure 3.24 shows the

HLS device being used to scan a statue, and a view of the computer-generated data. The resolution of the system is typically 0.50 mm at a range of 200 mm, and the scanning speed is 50 lines/sec.

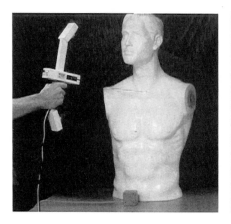

Fig. 3.24 *The Polhemus Hand-held Laser Scanner and computer model.*
(Image courtesy Polhemus)

Perspective view

We saw above how polygons and surface patches are used to represent 3D objects where the object's geometry is stored as vertices or CVs. The next stage is to derive a perspective view of this geometry from some specific position in space. To achieve this we need to locate the position of a virtual camera to view the animated objects.

Typically, a virtual camera has a position, viewing direction, roll rotation, and field of view. Its position is nothing more than a 3D point in space (X_c, Y_c, Z_c), as shown in figure 3.25. In the same figure, the camera's viewing direction is shown as an arrow, which mathematicians call a *vector*. Once the camera is positioned, it can be rotated about its viewing direction to create a degree of roll. Finally, the camera's field of view is adjusted to mimic a certain type of lens: wide angle, normal, telephoto.

The first stage in calculating the perspective image is to convert the coordinates of every object from the XYZ axes of the *World Coordinate System* (WCS), to the axial system of the camera. Once the 3D coordinates of the objects have been computed with respect to the *Camera's Coordinate System* (CCS), they are then subjected to a simple projection technique to create a perspective view, and represented as a collection of 2D coordinates. This replicates the action of a pin hole camera. Thus a solid cube is converted into a flat image, as shown in figure 3.26.

As the camera can be positioned anywhere in relation to the objects being viewed, there is a real possibility that some objects will be behind the camera, as well as in front of the camera. In real life, any object behind a real camera is invisible, because light is unable to find its way into the lens and excite the photographic film. In computer graphics, the mathematics used to perform the perspective projection is oblivious to such physical constraints, and steps have to be taken to obscure objects behind the camera.

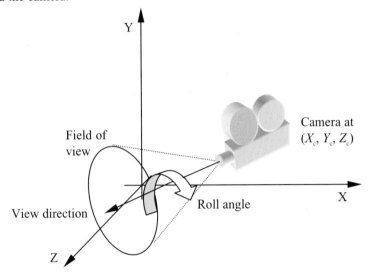

Fig. 3.25 *A camera's position, view direction, field of view and roll angle.*

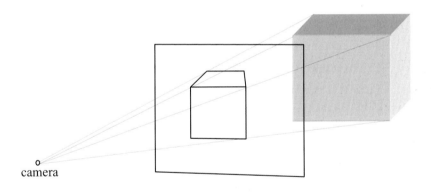

Fig. 3.26 *Creating a perspective view of a cube.*

3D clipping

Figure 3.27 depicts the camera's coordinate system where we see the camera looking along its Z-axis. Positioned on the Z-axis are two planes: the *near* and *far clipping planes*. These delimit the zone where objects are visible. For example, any object in front of the near plane is invisible, so too, is any object beyond the far plane. But any object between the near and far planes is visible. The near and far planes are called 'clipping' planes, as geometric techniques are used to clip objects that intersect these planes. The action of these planes is often visible in computer animations when the camera moves through a scene and intersects objects. The position of the planes is left to the animator, and can even be used to deliberately create an effect of cutting through an object like a bacon slicer. Whilst the near clipping plane solves the problem of removing objects too near to or behind the camera, the far clipping plane removes objects that are too far away from the camera, and are not rendered. The projection plane shown in figure 3.26 can be visualized to exist somewhere along the Z-axis in figure 3.27.

Objects outside the field of view of the camera are also clipped — that is above, below, to the left and to the right. This creates what is often called the *viewing frustum*, and has the form of a truncated pyramid, as shown in figure. 3.27.

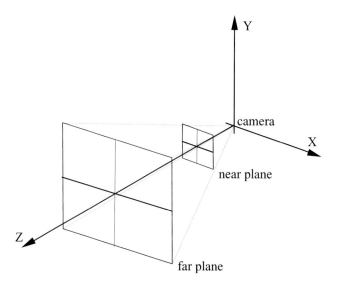

Fig. 3.27 *The viewing frustum formed by the near and far clipping planes.*

To illustrate how these clipping planes are used, consider the problem of placing a live actor inside a computer-generated, spherical, transparent space vehicle. The actor has to be seen through the glass but masked by the front detail of the vehicle, and in turn has to mask detail at the back of the vehicle. One solution is to render the vehicle in two stages: the first renders the sphere with the rear clipping plane at its center, so that its back half is removed. The second stage renders the sphere with the near clipping plane at its center, to remove its front. We now composite the three elements by starting with the back half of the sphere, followed by the live actor, followed by the front half of the sphere. This shot may have to be performed over a few dozen frames, and if the space vehicle is moving, the clipping planes will have to be adjusted for each frame.

Coordinate systems

Perhaps now is a good time to take a look at the coordinate systems used in computer animation. We already know that a 3D set of axes is used as a framework for locating objects in space, as depicted in figure 3.1. Such axes are used in association with 3D models, the camera, and the animation environment. In general, the virtual 3D world where everything takes place is called the *World Coordinate System* (X_{wcs}, Y_{wcs}, Z_{wcs}). In this world we place virtual objects, virtual lights and the virtual camera. To start with, objects are modeled in their own *Object Coordinate System* (X_{ocs}, Y_{ocs}, Z_{ocs}) and animated in the world coordinate system using various techniques. These axes are shown in figure 3.28.

The camera moves around the world coordinate system under the animator's control, and has its own local *Camera Coordinate System*. In order to calculate what the camera sees, the animation software has to recalculate every coordinate of every object and light source relative to the camera's axial system. Although this is a trivial mathematical calculation, it has to be done every time the camera or an object moves. In most computer animation this occurs on every frame, which means that the computer spends a lot of time simply recalculating the position of objects in the world coordinate system to the camera's coordinate system.

Fortunately, this conversion of coordinates from one system to another is transparent to the animator, but I have described it as you need to know why even very fast computers may take many seconds or minutes to render complex images.

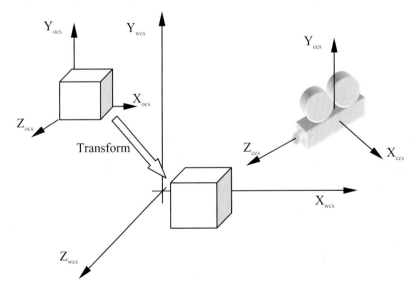

Fig. 3.28 *The world, camera and object coordinate systems.*

Transformations

When an object is modeled its coordinates are relative to its own local set of axes, as depicted in figure 3.28. It is then positioned in the world coordinate system by the animator. The animator may decide to alter the object's size or its orientation before selecting the object's resting place. Behind the scenes, computer software is storing these moves as *transformations*, which are mathematical operations for scaling, rotating and positioning objects. This term is often used in computer animation systems, and simply describes the way an object's coordinates are to be manipulated. For example, if we double the value of an object's coordinates its size doubles. Similarly, if we halve the value of the coordinates, its size halves. But if we add 10 just to the X-coordinates, it effectively moves 10 units along the X-axis. Transformations are at the heart of computer animation, and provide the mechanism for sliding, rotating, scaling and bending objects into new positions. We will return to this topic in the next chapter.

Rendering the image

The next stage is to render the perspective view in the form of a colored image comprised of *pixels*. These are discrete rectangular, picture elements that make up any picture shown on a television screen. But before we investigate the techniques for producing such an image, let's take a quick look at the color theory used in this process.

Color

Research has shown that the human eye samples the visible electromagnetic spectrum in three overlapping frequency bands with maximum sensitivities in red, green and blue. These colors have been adopted as the three *additive primary colors* for mixing light sources, whilst yellow, cyan and magenta are the corresponding *subtractive primary colors* for mixing paint pigment.

Computer technology uses mixtures of red, green and blue (RGB) to describe color and it is convenient to specify a color as three numbers that range from 0 to 1 to represent levels of red, green and blue. Thus an RGB triplet of (0, 0, 0) represents black and (1, 1, 1) represents white. Table 3.2 shows other values for RGB triplets and the corresponding color, and figure 3.29 provides a spatial way of interpreting this RGB data.

Although a color can be represented as an RGB triplet it is not very intuitive, and it is difficult to search for a specific color simply by adding or subtracting different amounts of red, green and blue. In an attempt to resolve this problem the HSV color space is also used to represent the quantities hue, saturation and value. To begin with, a number between 0 and 1 determines a particular hue; then saturation, which also varies between 0 and 1, controls the amount of white light in the color; and finally, a third value represents the brightness of the mixed color.

Figure 3.30 illustrates the HSV color space. As both systems have their respective strengths, they are both used in user interfaces to describe color.

Table 3.2 *Values of red, green and blue and the resulting color.*

Red	Green	Blue	Color
0	0	0	Black
0	0	1	Blue
0	1	0	Green
0	1	1	Cyan
1	0	0	Red
1	0	1	Magenta
1	1	0	Yellow
1	1	1	White

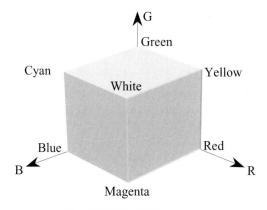

Fig. 3.29 *The RGB color space.*

Colored objects

After an object is modeled it is assigned a color. This may be selected from a given palette of colors or a particular mix of the video primary colors: red, green and blue. The entire model may have one color, or it may be that different sides or polygons have specific colors — virtually anything is possible.

The renderer uses the perspective view of an object to determine which pixels have to be painted, and the object's color is used to determine the RGB levels of the relevant pixels. The image can be made to look life-like by coloring the object with color shades that give the impression it is lit by some imaginary light source. Another way is to let the renderer automatically work out the surface shading of the object. To do this, the renderer is given the position and intensity of virtual light sources, and using some simple laws of illumination, shades the object with appropriate color intensities.

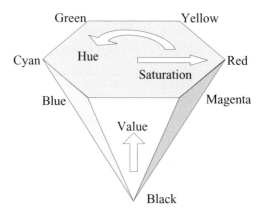

Fig. 3.30 *The HSV color space.*

Light sources

Light sources include ambient, spot, point, parallel and area. Ambient light is a background light level that has color and intensity, but no direction. It is included in the lighting calculations as a constant term and may account for approximately 25% of the total illumination level. A virtual spotlight simulates the action of its real-world counterpart and has position, direction, spot angle, color and intensity. A point light source is a point in space that radiates light in all directions, such as a light bulb, and a parallel light source shines light in one direction as though it were located at some distant position like the Sun.

Unfortunately, none of these light sources behave like their real-world counterparts: the Sun appears as a circular disk in the sky and radiates energy over an area. Similarly, a spotlight is not a point source of light energy — it radiates light from a reflector that has a measurable area. Various techniques have been investigated to create an area source of light, and radiosity is the most successful. But one simple solution is to organize a collection of discrete light sources in the form of a grid, and compute the collective light intensity illuminating an object. Obviously this takes extra time to compute, but it does give rise to more realistic shading. Together, these sources of light create realistic levels of illumination, but nowhere near as accurate as the radiosity technique.

Illumination models

In order to create an image with accurate colors and levels of illumination, various *illumination models* have been developed to simulate what happens in the real world. In reality, photons of light energy move through space at the speed of light, and their energy — often described as a frequency — is interpreted as color by our eyes. When a photon hits an object it is absorbed by a local electron and eventually ejected. The ejected photons give rise to all sorts of phenomena such as reflections, refraction, matte surfaces, interference, etc. There is no way that we can simulate the complex behavior of a photon-electron exchange in a computer animation system, therefore it is represented by a simple equation that describes the relationship between the light incident to a surface and the reflected light. Basically, there are four illumination models to consider: *ambient, diffuse, specular* and *Blinn*.

Ambient light

Ambient light is considered as a background level of light where photons are dancing around with all sorts of frequencies (colors). The photons move about randomly and consequently have no bias towards any direction. When they strike a surface they may be absorbed by an electron and used to heat up the object; but if the photon is ejected straight away, it will appear to obey the standard laws of reflection. The ambient illumination model has to show that for a given level of ambient light, some objects will reflect light better than others. An *ambient-reflection coefficient*, which ranges from 0 to 1, is used to control the amount of reflected light: when it is 0 no ambient light is reflected; and when it is 1 all ambient light is reflected. Furthermore, because computer graphics programs divide light into three primary bands: red, green and blue, there are three ambient-reflection coefficients. This enables ambient light to be set to any color and to interact with objects of different colors. For example, a tomato may have its ambient-reflection coefficients set to red = 1, green = 0.1, and blue = 0.1. When it is illuminated with white light (equal amounts of red, green and blue) the reflected ambient light will be in proportion to the coefficients: 100% red, 10% green, and 10% blue, and will look like a red tomato. However, if it is illuminated with blue ambient light, (red = 0, green = 0, and blue = 1) the reflected ambient light will only contain blue light, with no red or green component, and the tomato will look dark blue.

Diffuse reflection

The color and brightness of some surfaces depends upon the viewing direction. For example, velvet carpet is woven in such a way that its pile is biased, and its perceived color is influenced by the position of the viewer. However, a twist carpet has its tufts of wool pointing in all sorts of directions and its surface basically looks the same from all viewing angles. Matte paints create a similar effect by covering a surface with a colored layer that reflects light randomly. Such surfaces are called *diffuse surfaces* as they exhibit *Lambertian reflection*. The scientist Lambert discovered that the brightness of a diffuse surface is independent of the viewing angle, but is proportional to the intensity and the angle of the incident light. The angle is measured between the incident light and a datum line vertical to the surface. Mathematicians call the vertical datum line a *normal vector*. When the angle between the normal vector and the incident light is zero (i.e. overhead) the surface appears bright; and as the light source becomes increasingly oblique, the surface brightness dims to zero when the angle is 90°. Figure 3.31 illustrates this relationship.

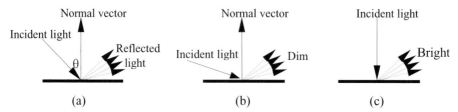

Fig. 3.31 *(a) The reflected light is proportional to the intensity of the incident light and the angle θ. (b) When θ is large the reflected light is dim. (c) When θ is zero the reflected light is bright.*

Light-source attenuation

The brightness of an object is measured by the number of photons leaving the surface in a given period of time. As they journey through space the photons are distributed over an ever-increasing surface area. The end result is that the perceived brightness of an object reduces with distance. The actual physical relationship is that the energy from a point light source falls off as the inverse square of the traveled distance. However, if this inverse square law is implemented within a computer animation system, we find that the resulting images are far from satisfactory. This is because, in reality, there are very few point sources of light, and the illumination models are far more complex than those used in computer graphics. As a compromise, researchers have designed an alternative model, which produces acceptable results.

Atmospheric attenuation

When photons leave an object they encounter all sorts of collisions and interactions as they fly through the atmosphere towards our eyes. Those photons that collide with this molecular debris may simply be used to increase its temperature, and are never seen again. The end result is that the perceived brightness of the object is attenuated with distance. This attenuation is a useful form of depth cueing, and is easily controlled by the animator. What happens in practice is that objects are subjected to a linear attenuation in brightness between a near and far distance.

Specular reflection

Specular reflections describe reflections of light sources that are seen on any polished or wet surface. Take, for example, a wet tomato. When we hold it in our hand we would see in its surface the reflection of kitchen ceiling lights, whose clarity and intensity would depend upon the reflective qualities of the tomato's skin. The very existence of the reflection of a light source in the skin reminds us that the surface is either polished or wet. But just try masking this reflective highlight with a finger, and straight away the tomato regains its normal matte luster.

If we gaze obliquely into a mirror, we see reflections of neighboring objects. And the more obliquely we gaze, the more offset the objects become. This is summarized in the law of incidence and reflection for a perfect reflector, where the angle of reflection equals the angle of incidence (figure 3.32).

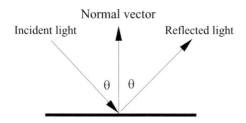

Fig. 3.32 *For a perfect reflector the angle of reflection equals the angle of incidence.*

The Phong illumination model

The nature of specular reflections depends entirely upon the quality of the reflective surface. For mirrors, the reflections are clear and precise, but for polished metallic surfaces they are less distinct and are spread over a small area. The dispersion of the highlight over an area is readily simulated in computer graphics, and enables surfaces of differing gloss factors to be created. Figure 3.33 shows how the reflected light is still seen over an angle of $\pm\alpha°$. When α is very small, the reflective highlight is correspondingly small, and the surface looks glossy. As the angle α increases, the highlight increases and the surface becomes increasingly metallic-like. Phong Bui-Tuong (Bui-Tuong 1975) developed the first algorithm for simulating this specular phenomenon, and his name has been associated with the illumination model ever since.

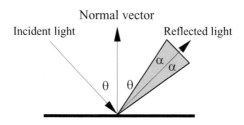

Fig. 3.33 *For an imperfect reflector the reflected light is seen over a wider reflective angle.*

The Blinn illumination model

James Blinn has made a significant contribution to computer graphics, especially in the area of anti-aliasing, bump mapping and rendering. He developed an illumination model that simulates the behavior of light with different metallic surfaces, which is incorporated in some computer animation systems.

Shading models

A shading algorithm describes how a polygon or surface patch is shaded, perhaps using one of the above illumination models. Various shading techniques have been developed over the years and include constant, interpolated, Gouraud and Phong shading.

Constant shading
Constant shading is a very simple shading model that fills an entire polygon with one color using an illumination model. The end result creates a very 'flat' effect, hence its other name *flat shading*.

Interpolated shading
Interpolated shading develops the constant shading algorithm by computing the light intensities at the vertices of a triangle, which are then used to interpolate the colors across the triangle's interior. Although this bears no relationship to what happens in reality, it is a real improvement on constant shading.

Gouraud shading
Both constant and interpolated shading fills individual triangles or polygons with color and leaves an object looking faceted. However, Gouraud developed a technique, *Gouraud shading*, that makes a faceted object look smooth (Gouraud 1971). Gouraud realized that as a polygon's surface normal vector is used by an illumination model to compute the reflected light intensity, it could be used to hide the edges between a pair of polygons. The algorithm first calculates an *average normal vector* at each vertex using the individual normal vectors as shown in figure 3.34. These *average vertex normals* are then used by the illumination model to calculate the reflected light, and because neighboring polygons share common average vertex normals, the boundary edge virtually disappears.

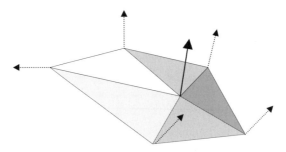

Fig. 3.34 *The center arrow is an average normal vector for the five surface normals represented by the dashed arrows.*

Although Gouraud shading hides the faceted nature of an object's surface, the silhouette always reveals the polygonal edges. But because the human visual system is sensitive to rapid changes in light intensity, the edge that Gouraud shading is trying to hide, can reappear as a highlight called *Mach bands*. This is particularly obvious when the edge is shared by polygons having disparate orientations.

Phong shading

As described above, interpolation shading uses the light intensities calculated at a polygon's vertices to blend color over its interior. In 1973 Phong Bui-Tuong proposed that the average surface normals used by Gouraud could be interpolated instead. This would enable the Phong illumination model to be applied at each pixel and reveal specular highlights. The extra computation meant that rendering time increased, but the increased realism was worthwhile.

Rendering algorithms

All renderers are faced with the problem of forming a picture such that objects mask one another correctly. In the field of computer graphics this is known as *hidden surface removal*. A number of algorithms (techniques) have been developed over the years such as Z-buffering, the scan-line algorithm, painter's algorithm, ray tracing, the A-buffer, etc., and they all have strengths and weaknesses. It will be impossible to cover them all in any depth, so I will concentrate on the scan-line, Z-buffer, ray tracing and radiosity.

Scan-line algorithm

A video image is transmitted and displayed on a television screen in the form of horizontal *rasters* or *scan-lines*, which is where the scan-line algorithm gets its name. The scan-line algorithm renders the image raster by raster, normally starting at the top, and working its way down to the bottom of the image.

To visualize what is happening, imagine gazing at a scene through a horizontal slit as shown in figure 3.35, that is as wide as the image but vertically very thin. The algorithm first identifies the objects visible in the slit and proceeds to sort them in depth sequence and loads the raster of colors into memory. It then proceeds to the next raster down. But as this is so close to the scan-line above, there is a very good chance that the same objects are visible, and therefore the depth relationships are the same. If another object comes into view, very little work is needed to adjust for its presence.

This algorithm has also been mixed with other techniques such as the Z-buffer, to create various hybrid renderers.

Z-buffer algorithm

The *Z-buffer*, or *depth buffer* algorithm, avoids any kind of sorting by storing the depth of rendered polygons at a pixel level. Which means that if there are 768×576 pixels in the image, there is a corresponding piece of computer memory called the Z-buffer, to record the depth of the polygon covering each pixel. The letter 'Z' is chosen, as it is the Z-axis that points away from the camera when the depth calculations are made.

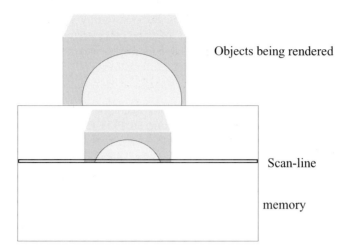

Objects being rendered

Scan-line

memory

Fig. 3.35 *Rendering an image using the scan-line algorithm.*

To visualize how this works, imagine that the Z-buffer is primed with very large depth values, such as 100,000. Say the first polygon to be rendered is 500 units away, every pixel it covers will be rendered and the corresponding positions in the Z-buffer updated with the value 500. If the next polygon to be rendered is 1,000 units away and is masked by the first polygon, the Z-buffer can be used to resolve the masking. For example, if the Z-buffer contains a depth value greater than 1,000 then the new polygon is visible. If, on the other hand, it contains a depth value less than 1,000, it means that a polygon has already been rendered that is closer.

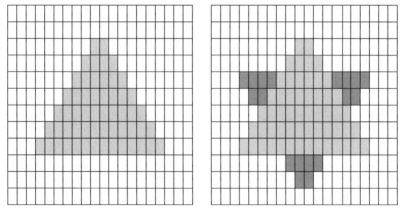

	Depth of 10,000
	Depth of 500
	Depth of 1,000

Fig. 3.36 *The two images show how the Z-buffer records the depths of the two polygons.*

Because depth is maintained at a pixel level, the Z-buffer can resolve interpenetrating objects. For example, if a small box intersected a larger sphere, the curves of intersection are revealed automatically by the Z-buffer, which saves an immense amount of modeling time. Z-buffering also allows simple animations to be made showing one object passing through another.

Although the Z-buffer is effective at hidden surface removal, the basic algorithm can not cope with transparency.

Texture mapping

If further realism is required, such as reflections, shadows, and spotlights, more advanced techniques are required. However, one quick way of incorporating extra realism is with the aid of *texture maps* (Catmull, 1974). These can be taken from photographs scanned into the computer or created by paint programs. For example, to make a virtual bookcase look more realistic, a photograph of wood grain can be scanned in and mapped onto the polygons by the renderer. Matching the scale of the texture to the size of the bookcase is important, and if the texture map is insufficient to cover a polygon, it can be repeated like a tile to ensure coverage. Figure 3.37 shows wire frame and textured view of a bookcase.

Fig. 3.37 A wire frame and a textured virtual bookcase.
(Image courtesy James Hans)

In the bookcase example, the texture map is projected onto each flat polygon as illustrated in figure 3.38. However, we know that objects can have curved surfaces, either using many small polygons or surface patches. And in such examples, different projection techniques are needed. For example, in figure 3.39, a cylindrical projection is used, and in figure 3.40, a spherical projection is used. Note that the texture becomes distorted by the mapping process, reminding us that a flat surface cannot be pasted onto a curved surface without being creased, stretched or torn in some way.

Mapping texture onto objects that remain close the observer is a very effective way of introducing extra detail, but problems arise when the object moves farther away. For example, if the object's size reduces by a factor of 5, the original texture is far too detailed. And if its size reduces by a factor of 10, another level of texture detail is required. This problem was appreciated by Lance Williams (Williams 1983) who proposed that a set of texture maps could be used to decorate objects at different distances. The name *MIP mapping* or *MIP textures* is given to this strategy. MIP textures also minimize aliasing artifacts that arise when *texels* (texture pixels) are mapped onto screen pixels.

Fig. 3.38 *Projecting texture maps onto flat polygons.*
(Image courtesy James Hans)

Dynamic textures

Dynamic textures are a sequence of texture maps applied to a surface in quick succession, and are used to simulate special effects such as flames, explosions and smoke trails.

Fig. 3.39 *Cylindrical projection of a texture map.*
(Image courtesy James Hans)

Fig. 3.40 *Spherical texture mapping.*
(Image courtesy James Hans)

Bump mapping

Another way of increasing image realism is *bump mapping*, developed by Jim Blinn (Blinn, 1978). Basically, it consists of using a texture map to modulate the way light is reflected, pixel by pixel. One would normally use photographs of bumpy materials such as concrete, leather, orange peel, etc., lit obliquely. Figure 3.41 shows how the original image (left) is interpreted by the renderer as a bumpy surface (right). This does not alter the geometry of the surface, only its appearance.

Fig. 3.41 *How a bump map is used to create a bumpy surface.*
(Image courtesy James Hans)

Environment mapping

Environment mapping (Blinn and Newell, 1976) simulates the effect of polished surfaces that reflect their surroundings. To a certain extent it is similar to texture mapping, but an environment map is not fixed to the object's surface — the image moves whenever the observer moves to create the impression of a reflection. It is particularly useful in the display of car bodies, and shows how reflective highlights travel over the surface of a moving car.

Figure 3.42 shows two views of a robot: the top one is flat shaded and the bottom one is environment mapped. The bottom image is much more realistic than the top one, and it becomes even more obvious when the robot is animated.

Displacement mapping

Displacement mapping (Cook, 1984) uses a reference image to physically displace the surface features of an object. For example, in figure 3.43 the reference image is shown on the left, and the resulting displaced surface is shown on the right. This is a very effective way of introducing extra surface geometry, without explicit modeling.

Fig. 3.42 *Two images of a robot: flat shaded (top)*
and environment mapped (bottom).
(Image courtesy James Hans)

Fig. 3.43 *Displacement mapping uses a displacement map (left)*
to create extra surface geometry (right).
(Image courtesy James Hans)

Shadows

Shadows in the real world just happen, but virtual shadows require considerable levels of computation. This is rather unfortunate because shadows do play an important role in the way we interpret the position and orientation of objects.

Various techniques have been developed to compute shadows, and they all require a geometric analysis of the spatial relationship between light sources and the objects in a scene. Ray tracing (see below) is particularly good at creating shadows, and in Fig. 3.44 we see the shadow cast by a sphere using such a technique. In fact, the shadow is too good, and rarely exists like this in the real world, as it requires a point light source. In reality, light sources such as the Sun, light bulbs and fluorescent tubes have an area, which bathes an object in light energy from different directions. This gives rise to an umbra and penumbra: the umbra is the central part of the shadow that receives no illumination, and the penumbra is partially illuminated. The overall effect gives rise to a soft shadow as shown in figure 3.45. This image is created using *softbox lighting*, where several light sources are directed onto the object. The term 'softbox' comes from photography where a subject is placed within a collection of diffuse reflective surfaces to create a homogeneous soft level of illumination. Obviously, this technique requires more time to compute, but the effect is very realistic.

Transparency

In the real world, photons can pass through materials such as glass, water and some plastics, and whenever they pass from one medium to another, such as air to glass, or water to air, their direction and speed are modified. This is called refraction, and is readily summarized by simple laws. Most transparent materials have some effect on any photons that attempt to pass through them: to begin with, some are reflected back at the boundary surface, and give rise to reflections. Those that penetrate the surface boundary may become absorbed by the medium and increase its temperature and change the overall color of the transmitted light. Other photons may be diverted along other paths and create *translucent* effects. Some may even be reflected away from the back of the transparent medium, and give rise to a second series of reflections. Those photons that manage to exit from the medium carry with them a history of their journey in the form of an altered color, intensity, polarization and direction.

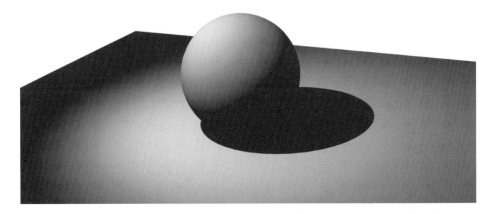

Fig. 3.44 *Sharp shadow using ray tracing.*
(Image courtesy James Hans)

Fig. 3.45 *Soft shadow using softbox lighting.*
(Image courtesy James Hans)

Transparency effects can be simulated with different levels of realism: from showing one polygon seen through another, modified by an appropriate color change, to realistic reflections, color and intensity changes and refraction. Unfortunately for the designers of rendering algorithms, we are very familiar with the way light behaves with transparent materials and notice when a computer image contains inaccurate optical effects.

Radiosity

Radiosity is a global illumination model that realizes photo-realistic images, and achieves them by simulating the internal reflections that arise when an interior is illuminated by light sources. These are represented as a series of equations that are solved to find a common solution, which can take anything from a few seconds to minutes or hours — much depends upon the complexity of the model.

Progressive refinement is another way of solving the radiosity model. It begins by looking at the brightest source of light and distributes its energy throughout the model. It then selects the next brightest source and continues to repeat the algorithm until changes in the image are too small to notice.

Ray tracing

The technique of ray tracing simulates, to a certain extent, the behavior of light energy in the real world. For example, we know that a light source such as the Sun, emits energy in the form of photons at the speed of light (300,000 Km/sec) that are absorbed by surfaces and reflected back into space and eventually into our eyes. What is amazing about the process is that even after many reflections the photons carry information about intensity and color that can be used to create an image. Various laws have been discovered that describe the actions of light emission, reflection and refraction, which can be simulated within a computer.

Figure 3.46 shows how the paths of photons can be traced to form an image. The scene shows the side view of a virtual camera recording the image projected onto a screen formed from pixels. The pixels are considered to be so small that only one ray can pass through, and it is this ray's history that is traced in the virtual world on the left. I have deliberately kept the virtual world very simple: it consists of a Sun, a blue box, a red sphere and a background color. To begin with, the ray-tracing program only considers a single pixel at a time, and traces the spatial origins of the photons that influence the pixel.

If we trace a ray from the camera back through any pixel three things can happen: the ray could hit the cube or sphere; it could hit the Sun, or it could miss everything. For example, ray A misses everything and will be assigned some background color, many rays will fall into this category. Ray B intersects the blue box, but by applying the geometric laws of reflection we can discover from where the reflected photons came. In fact, we see that it came from the Sun. This means that ray B consists of photons coming from the Sun, striking the blue box and reflecting through the middle pixel. The pixel's color will be the color of the Sun. Ray C, on the other hand, consists of a ray coming from the direction of the camera, through a pixel and striking the red sphere. But this is a reflected ray from the blue box, and the pixel's color is set to blue.

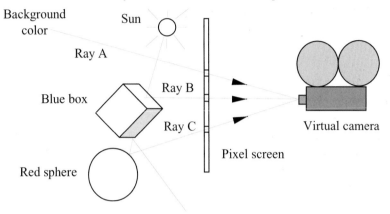

Fig. 3.46 *A side view of rays being traced through 3 pixels.*

The resulting image will contain reflections of the Sun in the sphere and box; reflections of the box in the sphere, and vice versa; and the background color. In fact, depending on how deep we are willing to trace the history of the photons, we could create reflections of objects that have reflections of other objects and light sources.

Ray tracing programs can be made very small as their only task is to determine the color of one pixel. But as the program has to be repeated for every pixel in the image, it can be a time-consuming process. However, modern implementations of this algorithm are very efficient, and create wonderful photo-realistic images.

As well as reflections, ray tracing also reveals the casting of shadows, transparency and refraction through water and glass. Figure 3.47 shows a collection of spheres standing on the obligatory computer-generated chessboard. Although the image is much more realistic than simple rendering techniques, it is still too hard, but can be softened using a combination of radiosity and ray tracing as shown in figure 3.48.

Because ray tracing employs a geometric approach to the behavior of light, it can be used to simulate the optical characteristics of a lens. Normally, renderers just assume that light rays pass through a mathematical pinhole before being used to render a perspective view. But in reality, this is not true. Real cameras have lenses, which possess all sorts of optical characteristics such as a field of view, a focal length, and a depth of field. Wide-angle lenses not only provide a wide viewing angle; they also introduce distortion across the image, and emphasize the size of objects that come very close. Therefore, if computer-generated images are to look similar to those captured by real cameras, they must include the optical features associated with a lens. Compound lenses introduce lens flares caused by unwanted inter-reflections, which are deliberately included by computer animators to fool the viewer into accepting their animation as photorealistic!

Fig. 3.47 *Ray traced spheres showing reflections and shadows.*
(Image courtesy James Hans)

Fig. 3.48 *Three spheres rendered using ray tracing and radiosity.*
(Image courtesy James Hans)

One natural feature of a lens is its depth of field. This is the optical depth where the image is in focus. Outside of this region the image is out of focus. A ray tracing renderer easily simulates this, and an example is shown in figure 3.49.

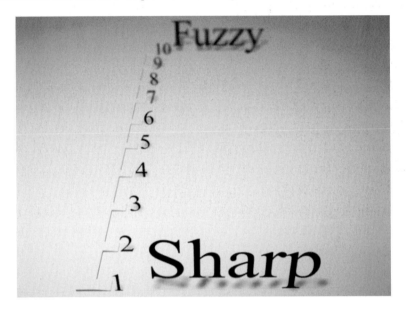

Fig. 3.49 *Depth of field simulated by ray tracing.*
(Image courtesy James Hans)

Volumetric lighting

As light is only perceived when it strikes an object, the space between objects is normally invisible. However, conditions can arise when the space is made visible especially when the air holds moisture, dust or smoke. For example, when sunlight illuminates the interior of a cathedral, shafts of light are readily seen by internal moisture and dust. Such effects can be recreated using volumetric lighting, and an example is shown in figure 3.50. The illustration shows a light source on the left, which illuminates the volume of space. The illuminated sphere also casts a shadow through the atmosphere.

Shaders

You will have seen from the above sections that all sorts of techniques have been developed to improve the realism of computer generated images, and perhaps you may have realized that we will never reach a point when we can render everything. There will always be something that demands a new technique. This presents serious problems for the designers of computer animation software, as they have to provide their users with a renderer that can render a wide range of surface finishes. As this is currently impossible, they allow users to 'plug-in' extra software modules that undertake a specific task. *Plug-ins* for a renderer are known as *shaders*, and are programs that are called during the rendering phase to perform a specific task. For example, a shader could be used to create a brick pattern over a polygon. Because the pattern is regular, it is relatively easy to describe a logical procedure that spaces rectangles in a brick fashion, leaving room for the mortar (figure 3.51).

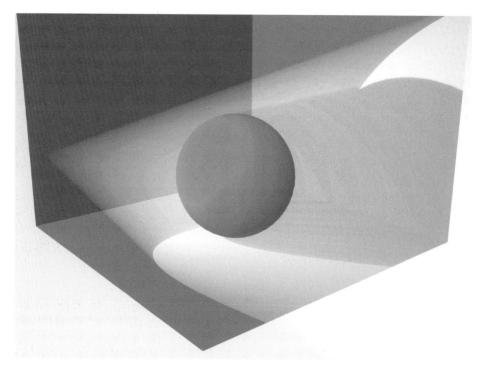

Fig. 3.50 *Volumetric lighting for illuminating a volume of space.*
(Image courtesy James Hans)

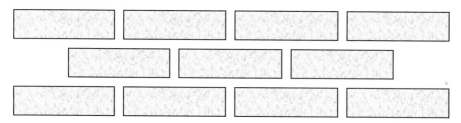

Fig. 3.51 *A brick pattern created by a procedure.*

The shader will be given the horizontal and vertical dimensions of a brick, the spacing for the mortar, and the texture to be used. But as it is a procedure, rather than a large texture map, it can be used to decorate any surface with this pattern, no matter how large it is. Naturally, shaders present a powerful way to decorate surfaces, and played a very important role in films such as *Antz* and *A Bug's Life*.

Shaders are used to create all sorts of effects such as marble, sea states, clouds, mist, smoke, fire, waves, bumps, cracks, dirt, etc., but someone has to design a procedure in the first place, which is a non-trivial exercise. Darwyn Peachey (Ebert, 1998) lists the following advantages and disadvantages:

Advantages

- A procedural representation is extremely compact. The size of a procedural texture is usually measured in kilobytes, while the size of a texture image is usually measured in megabytes. This is especially true for solid textures, since 3D texture maps are extremely large. Nonetheless, some people have used tomographic X-ray scanners to obtain digitized volume images for use as solid textures.
- A procedural representation has no fixed resolution. In most cases it can provide a fully detailed texture no matter how closely you look at it (no matter how high the resolution).
- A procedural representation covers no fixed area. In other words, it is unlimited in extent and can cover an arbitrarily large area without seams and without unwanted repetition of the texture pattern.
- A procedural texture can be parameterized, so it can generate a class of related textures rather than being limited to one fixed texture image.

Disadvantages

- A procedural texture can be difficult to build and debug. Programming is often hard, and programming an implicit pattern description is especially hard in non-trivial cases.
- A procedural texture can be a surprise. It is often easier to predict the outcome when you scan or paint a texture image. Some people choose to like this property of procedural textures and call it serendipity. Some people hate it and say that procedural textures are hard to control.
- Evaluating a procedural texture can be slower than accessing a stored texture image. This is the classic tradeoff between time and space.
- Aliasing can be a problem in procedural textures. Anti-aliasing can be tricky and is less likely to be taken care of automatically that it is in image-based texturing.

The RenderMan Shading Language

Shaders can be defined using the RenderMan Shading Language, which was developed to simplify their design. It provides an interface where a shader is specified in a C-like computer language and supports six types of shader: light source, volume, transformation, displacement, surface and image.

- A light source shader computes the color of the light originating in the light source and striking a surface point.
- A volume shader computes the effects of light passing through a volume of space from an origin to a destination.
- A transformation shader is used to modify geometry rather than affect surface color, and uses a point in space to determine a new point.
- A displacement shader is used to perturb the surface of an object point by point, creating surface detail without any new geometry.
- A surface shader computes how light interacts with a surface, and how it is finally reflected.
- An image shader is used to convert the numbers describing a pixel-based image into another description.

To give the reader a flavor of what a shader looks like, Appendix B contains a shader reproduced from Steve Upstill's excellent book *The RenderMan Companion* (Upstill, 1989).

Aliasing

Video images often contain artifacts that betray the raster nature of video technology (figure 3.52). Likewise, computer-generated images often contain artifacts that betray their pixel structure. Such artifacts appear in the form of jagged edges or irregular patterns on moving texture and are called *aliasing*. Figure 3.53 shows how the jagged edges arise when a polygon is rendered using a simple renderer. Because pixels are sampled at their center to see if they are covered by the polygon, partially covered pixels may or may not be rendered. For example, if the polygon just covers the center, it will be rendered. But if it misses the center by the smallest distance, it is not.

Fig. 3.52 *Part of a video image showing aliasing artifacts.*

The problem is that it is impossible to partially fill a pixel — it must be assigned a single color. So edges and small polygons will always give rise to such aliasing artifacts, unless something is done to disguise them. Such strategies, called *anti-aliasing* techniques, reduce the visual impact of aliasing artifacts by more sophisticated sampling methods.

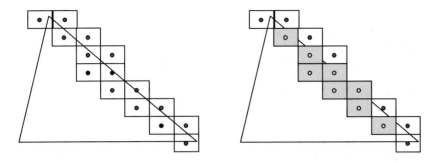

Fig. 3.53 *A pixel is sampled at its center (left), and rendered accordingly (right).*

Anti-aliasing

One anti-aliasing technique is to compute the area of the pixel covered by a polygon. For example, figure 3.54 shows a pixel covered completely by a bright red pentagon. If a bright green triangle overlaps the same pixel by 50%, an anti-aliasing algorithm would set the pixel yellow (50% red and 50% green). The resulting effect is to replace sudden changes from red to green pixels, with pixels containing different mixtures of red and green.

More sophisticated anti-aliasing techniques apply a more rigorous mathematical analysis to this computation, and are beyond the scope of this text.

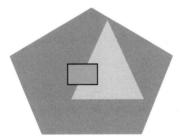

Fig. 3.54 *The color of a pixel is determined by percentage overlap of polygons.*

Conclusion

There has only been space to cover this subject at a very superficial level. If one attempts to go any deeper it is necessary to employ mathematics. Nevertheless, the terms that have been introduced are widely used in computer animation GUIs, and if you have understood the general principles that have been discussed, you will find it much easier to work with a commercial animation system.

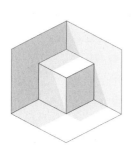

4
Computer Animation Techniques

Introduction

Animation, whether it is traditional or computer-generated, is about movement — moving characters, moving objects, moving cameras, moving lights and moving special effects. Traditional animators rely upon their drawing skills to endow a cartoon character with life-like movement; as they are not constrained by any physical laws, movements can be accentuated and shapes distorted to achieve an effect. Computer animators, on the other hand, rely upon software to realize movement. And although they still require an 'eye' for motion, they have a wide range of software aids at their disposal to perfect their animation.

In cartoon animation the moving image is frozen as a series of images on paper or cel, and can only be realized by flicking through the images or recording them and playing back the animation. Understandably, it is a laborious process, but nevertheless it is very successful. Computer animation is still a laborious process, but instead of storing images on a physical medium, they are stored digitally, which enables them to be manipulated, modified and composited with other images with reasonable ease.

The real difference, however, between cartoon and computer animation is that a cartoon animator draws each image to develop a moving character, whereas a computer animator models a 3D character once, and develops a script to move the model. The computer is then used to render views of the character at appropriate stages of the script.

In this chapter we are going to explore some of the techniques used in computer animation to make things move, be they characters, objects, cameras, lights or special effects. Ultimately, these techniques have a mathematical origin, but any good animation system will hide such notation from the user. The GUI used by the computer animator will present various graphs, sliders, buttons and menus that simplify the animation process.

We have already seen that objects and characters are built from collections of vertices or CVs, which are represented by numbers; and if these numbers are changed in a consistent manner, the object or character will appear to move or alter in size. Therefore, making numbers change is central to computer animation, and is the first topic of this chapter.

Interpolation

There are many ways of changing one number into another. For example, the number 5 could be changed into 10 in five steps by repeatedly adding 1 to it; i.e. 5, 6, 7, 8, 9, 10. We could also change 5 into 10 in two steps by repeatedly adding 2.5 to it; i.e. 5, 7.5, 10. But say we wanted to change 5 into 10 in six steps; we would require a formula to find the number such that when repeatedly added to 5 resulted in 10. In fact, the number is 0.833, which gives: 5, 5.833, 6.666, 7.5, 8.333, 9.166, 10.

As animators, we do not want to worry about formulae — nevertheless, we still require to control the speed with which one number changes into another, because this will determine how fast our computer-generated characters will move. So instead of using pure numbers, we use graphs, which are far less intimidating.

Now the technique of calculating a value between two numbers is called *interpolation*, and this can be specified as a percentage. For example, 50% between 0 and 20 is 10; 25% is 5; and 75% is 15. Table 4.1 shows further percentage values, and figure 4.1 shows the relationship as a graph.

***Table 4.1** Interpolated values between 0 and 20.*

%	Value
0	0
10	2
20	4
30	6
40	8
50	10
60	12
70	14
80	16
90	18
100	20

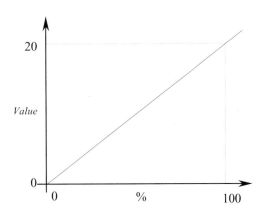

***Fig. 4.1** The graph of Value against %.*

The graph shows that the change in *Value* is directly proportional to the *Percentage* (%) and produces the straight-line relationship. Mathematicians call this a *linear*, or a *first degree* graph. This type of numeric calculation is second nature to a computer, and could easily be used to control the position of a camera. For instance, if we located a camera at position xyz = (10, 0, 20) for frame 1, and xyz = (20, 10, 30) for frame 11, software could calculate the interpolated values between the two positions. These have been computed and are shown in table 4.2. We see at frame 1 the camera's position is (10, 0, 20), and at frame 11 it is (20, 10, 30). But we can also see that at frame 4 the position is (13, 3, 23) and at frame 7 it is (16, 6, 26). To animate the camera we program the computer with the initial position of the camera, i.e. xyz = (10, 0, 20), and its final position, xyz = (20, 10, 30). The animation software then computes the first interpolated value, positions the camera at this point, renders the image and stores it to disk. This process is repeated for subsequent frames until frame 11 is produced.

Now I chose these numbers very carefully to ensure that there were no fractional values, but this is not a problem for a computer. As one would expect, a computer can calculate numbers to a very high precision, which means that it can be programmed to interpolate the first camera position to the second camera position over any number of frames.

Table 4.2 *Coordinate values of two camera positions.*

Frame	X	Y	Z
1	10	0	20
2	11	1	21
3	12	2	22
4	13	3	23
5	14	4	24
6	15	5	25
7	16	6	26
8	17	7	27
9	18	8	28
10	19	9	29
11	20	10	30

If we implemented the above animation sequence, we would notice that the camera suddenly moves from standstill, moves smoothly to the new position, and suddenly stops. This would look strange, for we know from our own personal experience of motion that it is difficult to suddenly move and suddenly stop. In order to change the speed of anything, we must do work — which requires energy. Furthermore, the heavier the object, the more work we must do. For example, consider the case of pushing a large automobile. It would be impossible to move it from a standstill instantaneously. It requires a sustained force to overcome its inertia and any frictional forces, and once it starts rolling a further force is needed to increase its speed. Similarly, it is impossible to stop the automobile suddenly. Further energy must be expended to slow it down over a period of time. Isaac Newton knew about this — even though automobiles had yet to be invented — and expressed it in the form of a universal law, which states that the acceleration of an object is directly proportional to the applied force, and inversely proportional to the object's mass. Thus large forces applied to light objects, result in high accelerations.

Let us now imagine that we conducted this experiment of pushing an automobile from standstill, maintaining its speed, and then stopping it. At the same time, someone recorded the automobile's speed at regular intervals. If we expressed this recorded data as a graph it could like the graph shown in figure 4.2.

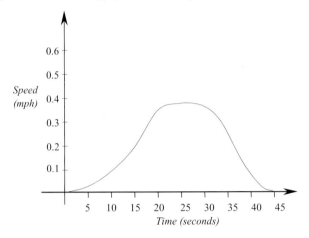

Fig. 4.2 *Graph of speed against time.*

The graph records what happened during the experiment: At time zero the speed of the automobile was zero. After 5 seconds it was barely moving; and even after 10 seconds it had still not reached 0.1 mph. By 15 seconds it was starting to roll nicely at just under 0.2 mph. By 20 seconds it had accelerated to about 0.35 mph. Between 20 and 30 seconds the pushing had stopped, and by 35 seconds it was starting to slow down. By 45 seconds, the automobile had been brought to a rest.

Now all of this can be interpreted from the slope of the graph: acceleration is when the graph curls up from a horizontal position to a higher speed; constant speed is a horizontal line; and deceleration is when the graph curls down to a lower speed. This means that graphs can be used to dictate how objects can be animated.

Function curves

To illustrate the application of graphs in computer animation, let us return to the exercise above of interpolating one number into another. Instead of linearly interpolating between two numbers, which graphically is a straight line, let us introduce some acceleration and deceleration, as shown in figure 4.3. The graph shows time in terms of animation frames along the horizontal axis, and numeric value up the vertical axis. At frame 1 we see that the numeric value is zero, and at frame 11 it is 20. But there is no longer a linear relationship between frames and value — it is definitely a *non-linear* relationship.

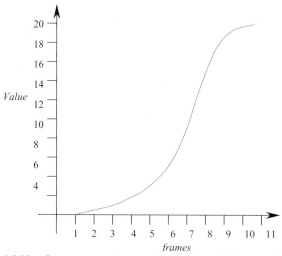

Fig. 4.3 *Non-linear interpolation between 0 and 20 over 11 frames.*

We see from the graph that at frame 2 there has only been a very small change in value, and there is a gradual acceleration up until frame 7, where it becomes linear. But then the curve anticipates the deceleration needed to arrive at a value of 20 at frame 11 and curls down accordingly. In computer animation, such a graph is called a *function curve*, or *f–curve* for short. It is extremely useful as it enables an animator to control all sorts of motion just by using a graph. And by changing the slope of the graph, one has total control of accelerations and decelerations.

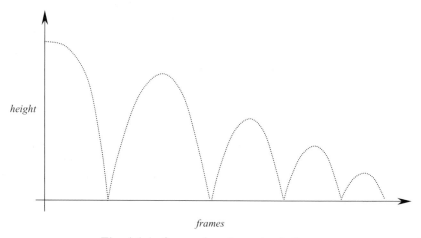

Fig. 4.4 *An f-curve for a bouncing ball.*

To illustrate this further, one could animate a bouncing ball using the f-curve shown in figure 4.4. The vertical axis represents the height of the ball for any frame. We can see from the graph that the ball accelerates downwards, hits the ground and bounces upwards to repeat the cycle. Successive bounces are not only smaller but occur faster, which is what happens in reality. If after playing back the animation we are unhappy with the way the bounces die away, we can return to the f-curve, and modify it using the GUI.

Function curves are a very powerful animation tool for the animator as they can be applied in all sorts of situations. They can be used to slide objects about; make objects float up and down; spin objects about an axis; move a camera from one position to another; alter the brightness of a light source; or control the rate at which a flower opens its petals.

Parameters

Any number used to control or modify the status of something is called a *parameter*. Typical examples include angles, colors, displacements, CVs, positions, surface attributes, velocities, accelerations, etc. The animator sets such parameters when modeling an object, decorating its surface, or illuminating and animating a scene, and very often, default values can be set by the animation software to save time.

Computer animation, then, is all about changing parameters to make things move over a period of time. For example, if the position of an object is controlled by a parameter, specifying different parameter values for individual frames can animate the object. The parameter value can be derived from any source such as an f-curve, a program, a file, a mouse, or even a real-time electronic device.

It is convenient to divide parameters into two sets: *global* and *local parameters*. Global parameters, as one would expect, have a global impact upon the animation, and include things such as shading, fog, lights, camera, etc., and local parameters control the attributes of an object such as color, scale, translation, rotation angles, etc.

The animator has the option to identify as many parameters as is necessary to provide the control over the animation. Furthermore, GUI tools make it easy to change a parameter to perfect a specific piece of animation.

Channels

If a parameter represents a single datum, a *channel* is a set of data representing its values over a period of time. Such a data channel can be represented as a list of numbers or shown graphically as an f-curve. For any animation, many channels will be used to control global and local parameters.

Keyframes

Any animation sequence, whether it is traditional or computer-generated, is recorded as individual frames. The NTSC video frame rate in the USA is 30 frames per second (fps), whilst the PAL video rate in the UK is 25 fps. The film industry, generally, employs 24 fps, although higher frame rates are used for special film applications. To increase productivity in cel-based animation, a senior animator draws specific *keyframes*, and a junior animator fills in the missing *inbetween* frames. Whilst the keyframes provide the overall structure to the animation, the inbetween frames give the continuity and fluidity of movement. The same technique has been implemented in computer animation.

For each keyframe the animator places an object in a specific position, and identifies the keyframe number. The software extracts the local and global parameters of the keyframe so that they can be interpolated. The parameters will consist of joint angles in a skeleton; angles of rotation for an object; X, Y, and Z translations; light and camera positions, etc. After this, the animation is played back to observe the desired effect. For wire frame images, most computers can do this in real time, but for detailed rendered images, they will first have to be recorded to disk and then played back. If the animation contains any defects, the animator identifies the channel storing the relevant parameter data, modifies it and repeats the process until the animation is satisfactory.

At a software level, keyframe parameters are taken from the channel and interpolated to produce the inbetween frames. It is highly likely that keyframes will have to be moved, deleted, or even new ones inserted, and the GUI must make it easy to undertake such tasks. The GUI will allow the animator to cut, copy and paste keyframes into the same channel or the channel of another object. Most animation systems provide the animator with an interface that shows the range of frames animated, playback controls and a moving slider that identifies the displayed frame. Such an interface is shown in figure 4.5.

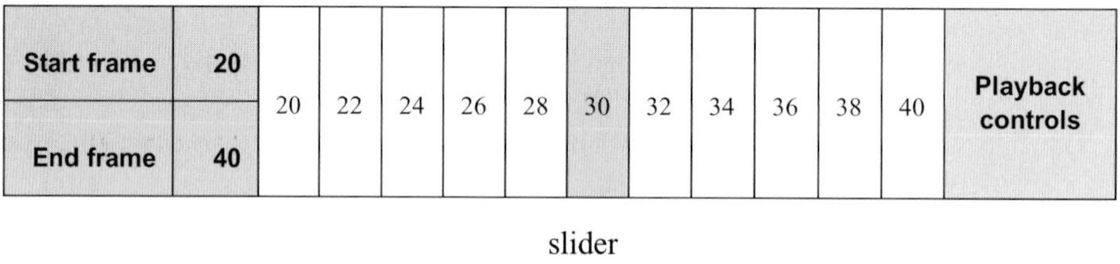

Start frame	20												Playback controls
		20	22	24	26	28	30	32	34	36	38	40	
End frame	40												

slider

Fig. 4.5 *A typical GUI used to playback an animation.*

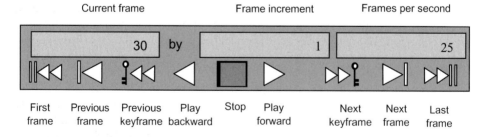

Fig. 4.6 *A typical GUI interface for controlling a keyframe animation system.*

On the left of figure 4.5, we see the *Start* and *End frames* of the animation, whilst in the central portion, a *slider* moves horizontally highlighting the current frame number. The *Playback controls* are similar to those found on a modern video recorder, as shown in figure 4.6. There are buttons to select the first, previous, last and next frame; to select the previous and next keyframes; to play backwards and forwards; and a stop button. The *Frames per second* window ensures that the system plays back the animation at the desired speed. This prevents the computer from displaying the images at some arbitrary speed. Such a GUI is vital to any animation interface.

Inbetweening

When interpolating numbers, we saw that they could be interpolated linearly or non-linearly. Linear interpolation looks very strange when used to move an object from standstill, or to bring an object to rest, and therefore non-linear interpolation is necessary to introduce accelerations and decelerations. Traditional animators call this *cushioning* or *slowing in* and *slowing out*.

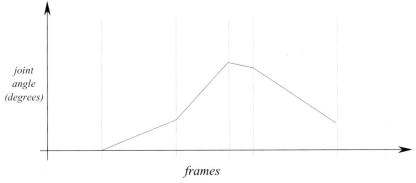

Fig. 4.7 Linear interpolation between keyframes.

In keyframe animation we need to specify the animation speed between a pair of keyframes. For example, we can move linearly (equal time steps), accelerate away from one keyframe, and decelerate into the next keyframe (non-linear steps), and other sorts of combinations. The most effective way of controlling this is with the aid of f-curves. Figure 4.7 shows a sequence of keyframes where, for example, a joint angle is inbetweened using linear interpolation. It is obvious from the joint angles that the resulting animation will appear very disjointed, with sudden motion changes.

To smooth out the mechanical motion that results from linear animation curves, we simply introduce a smooth curve. But although this creates smooth animation between pairs of keyframes, the overall animation may be interrupted by slight changes of speed between neighboring pairs of animation curves. This is illustrated in figure 4.8 where we notice a 'kink' at the join of the animation curves. One simple way of overcoming this is to define the curve slope at the keyframes, and ensure that the animation curves share this slope. Figure 4.9 identifies the discrete slopes at the keyframes, and the resulting curve is smooth and free from any kinks. The slopes or tangents shown in figure 4.9 may appear in a GUI as *tangency options*.

Another useful type of curve is called a *Hermite curve*, which actually passes through its control vertices, which makes it very easy to obtain a particular shape.

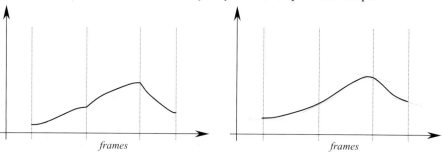

Fig. 4.8 *Smooth animation curves between keyframes, but with kinks at the keyframes.*

Fig. 4.9 *Smooth animation curves that share a common slope at the keyframes.*

Slow in/Slow out

Traditional animators create accelerations and decelerations by changing the number of drawings approaching or leaving a keyframe. In computer animation, this is controlled directly by the animation curves described above. Such curves are much more flexible, as they can be 'tweaked' until the desired movement is achieved.

Slow in means that the movement slows down (deceleration) as the keyframe is approached, and *slow out* that the movement speeds up (acceleration) out of the keyframe. A variety of animation curves are shown in figure 4.10.

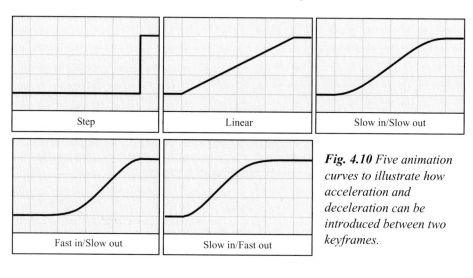

Fig. 4.10 *Five animation curves to illustrate how acceleration and deceleration can be introduced between two keyframes.*

Motion paths

In some types of animation an object or camera has to follow a specific path. For example, a circular or elliptical path is desired, or the motion of a real-world object has been supplied and must be replicated by the computer animation sequence. Such a 3D trajectory is called a *motion path*. In fact, anything can be forced to move along a motion path: an object, a camera, light or a CV.

Transformations

Hopefully, you are beginning to see that computer animation is based upon the manipulation of numbers to produce moving images. We have already discovered that 3D objects are nothing more than collections of numbers describing polygons, or surface patches defined by collections of CVs. But so far we have only briefly discussed how objects are actually animated, so let us now take a closer look at the subject of *transformations*.

Scaling transformation

As a 3D object is basically a file of X, Y and Z coordinates, its size is dictated by the magnitude of the coordinate values. Therefore, if we double all the numbers representing an object's coordinates, the object's size effectively doubles in all directions. But if we only double the X coordinates, the object's size will only double in the X direction. The same is true for the Y and Z coordinates. Thus changing the size of an object is a trivial operation for a computer. Even if an object consists of tens of thousands of coordinates, they can be resized in a fraction of second. Such an operation is called a *scaling transformation* (figure 4.11).

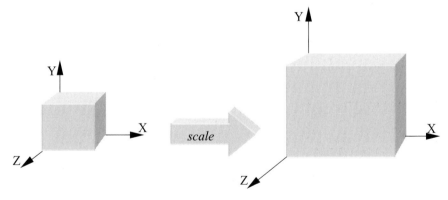

Fig. 4.11 *An object located at the origin will be scaled as shown.*

We could animate an object's size by specifying two key frames with different scaling parameters. Using a suitable animation curve, the size of the object would change as the animation moved between the two keyframes.

Translation transformation

Instead of multiplying the coordinates by some number, we could add a number to them. For example, if we increased all of the X coordinates by 0.1, it would effectively move the object to a new position 0.1 units along the X-axis. If this addition were to be repeated for 100 frames, the object would appear to be animated parallel with the X-axis, as shown in figure 4.12. Naturally, the Y and Z coordinates could be increased in a similar way, resulting in movement along the Y and Z-axes respectively. As computers perform additions and subtractions extremely fast (millions of operations per second), this *translation transformation* is very easy to compute.

We could animate an object's position between two keyframes using the same technique as for changing its size.

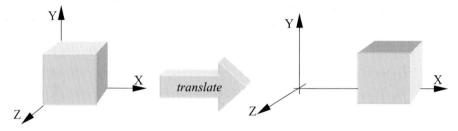

Fig. 4.12 Translating an object along the X-axis.

Rotation transformation

A third transformation called a *rotation transformation* is used to rotate an object about an axis. This transformation uses a branch of mathematics called *trigonometry* (triangles, sines, cosines and tangents) to manipulate the X, Y and Z coordinates such they can be rotated in space. Transformations are available to rotate an object about one of the three axes. Figure 4.13 illustrates a cube rotated about the X-axis.

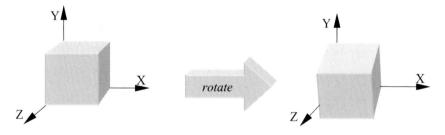

Fig. 4.13 Rotating an object about the X-axis.

In mathematics the direction of rotation is positive in an anti-clockwise direction, and negative in a clockwise direction. This presents no problems when working in 2D, but in 3D it depends upon the viewing direction of the observer. The convention used in computer graphics is to imagine one is looking along an axis towards the origin. A positive rotation is then anti-clockwise. In figure 4.13 the cube is rotating in a positive sense when looking along the X-axis.

To create more complex rotations, such as a tumble sequence, the animator has to combine rotations about the X, Y and Z-axes to create the desired effect — this is not always easy. To create a tumbling object, the object is subjected to a mixture of rotations about its local axes. But if an object has to rotate about another object, such as a planet moving around the Sun, it is rotated about the world frame of reference.

Hierarchical animation

The three transformations described above: scale, translation and rotation, play a fundamental role in animating objects in computer animation. However, it raises a very important issue concerning transform sequence. For example, is the sequence in which the transformations are applied important? Well, yes it is. To illustrate this phenomenon let us consider a 2D example shown in figure 4.14.

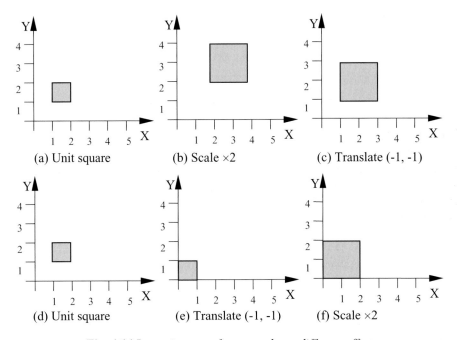

Fig. 4.14 *Reversing transforms produces different effects.*

Figure 4.14a shows a square of unit size offset from the origin by xy = (1, 1). Figure 4.14b shows the square scaled by a factor of 2, and we see that every coordinate is doubled, which not only doubles the square's size but also doubles its position from the origin. figure 4.14c shows the scaled square translated by xy = (-1, -1).

Figures 4.14d, 4.14e, and 4.14f show what happens when the transformations are changed from scale followed by translation, to translation followed by scale — they are not the same!

This example confirms that the transform sequence is very important in preparing an animation — reversing the order of the transforms creates a totally different result. Furthermore, this is even more complicated when rotation transformations are introduced. One should not be too concerned by this, for it is quite easy to see what is going on, and once it is understood, it is no longer an issue.

Computer animation systems anticipate these issues and force the animator to think in terms of a *transform hierarchy*. That is to say, for any object, the sequence of transforms must be specified explicitly so that there is no confusion; this is called *hierarchical animation*.

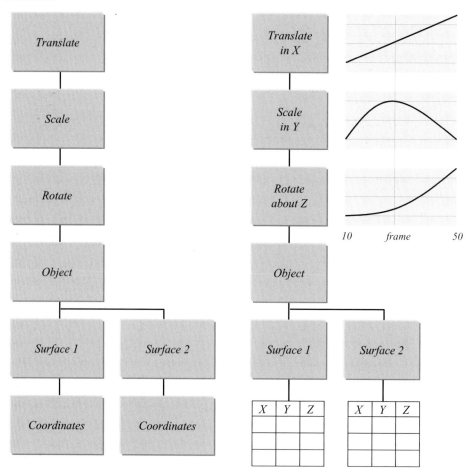

Fig. 4.15 *The hierarchical relationship between an object, its data, and transforms.*

Fig. 4.16 *How animation curves are used to extract a local parameter to drive a transform.*

To aid the animator the GUI provides a graphical description of the relationship between an object and its transforms. In figure 4.15 we see an object consisting of two surfaces, and their respective coordinates. The object is first subjected to a rotate transform, followed by a scale, and then a translation. Notice that the diagram forces us to express the transform sequence working upwards, away from the object.

The values for the transformations are often expressed as animation curves, where, for example, a curve depicts the translation for an object over a range of keyframes. For each frame, a translation parameter is read from the curve by the animation software and used to translate the object. Similar parameters are taken from animation curves controlling scaling and rotation. The object is animated by combining the transforms in a specific hierarchy. The hierarchy will always specify the transforms used by the animator and the sequence in which they are to be applied.

Figure 4.16 shows a hierarchy, together with some sample animation curves. Such animation is easily played back to the animator, who can adjust the animation curves and keyframes until a particular effect is achieved. In this example the animation curves depict how the object is to be rotated about the Z-axis, scaled in the Y direction, and translated in the X direction between the frames 10 to 50. For any frame, the coordinates comprising surfaces 1 and 2 are first rotated about the Z-axis; then scaled in the Y-axis; and finally translated along the X-axis. The new coordinates are used by the renderer to create an image, leaving the original coordinates unmodified.

Hierarchical geometry

A simple way of classifying objects is to divide them into two groups: those that have no moving parts and those that do. In the first group we include things such as a cube, ball, spoon, plate, cup, etc., and in the second group, things such as a hand, chest of drawers, dog, human, computer keyboard, etc. To animate objects in the first group we simply apply a series of transforms to the object's coordinates. But in the second group we must be able to identify every individual part of the object that moves relative to the object, as well as the entire object. For example, in the case of a human hand we need to move an individual finger without moving the other fingers. But when we move the complete hand, all the fingers must move together, otherwise the hand will have no geometric integrity. To support such animation we must construct our objects with a geometric hierarchy.

Figure 4.17 shows how we could organize the hierarchic geometry for a simple human character. We see that the body is divided into two sections: the *Upper body* and the *Lower body*, with a join at the waist. The *Upper body* comprises the *Chest, Right arm* and *Left arm*, whilst the *Lower body* comprises the *Abdomen, Right leg* and *Left leg*. This allows the character to stand with its feet firmly stuck to the ground, but by rotating the *Upper body* through a small angle, we can mimic a human-like twisting motion. If we rotate the coordinates of the character's *Left leg* about a hip joint it can be made to stand on one leg. But if the *Left lower leg* is first rotated about its knee joint, and the entire *Left leg* rotated about the hip joint, it will look as though it is about to climb a step. By creating this hierarchy of geometry it is possible to isolate individual elements, and groups of elements, as well as the entire structure.

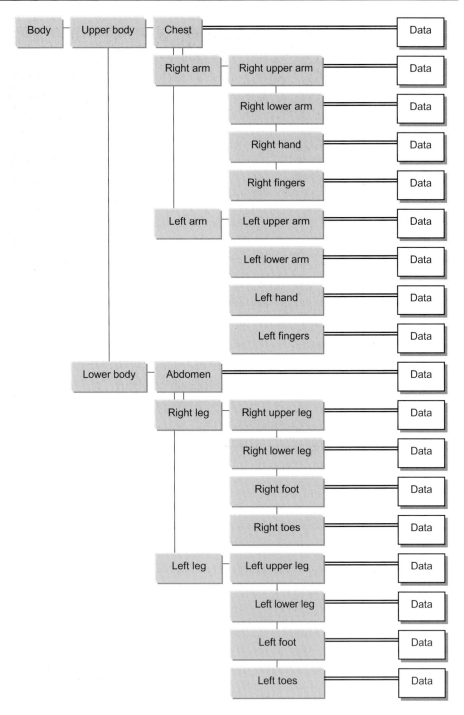

Fig. 4.17 *The hierarchical geometry for a simple human character.*

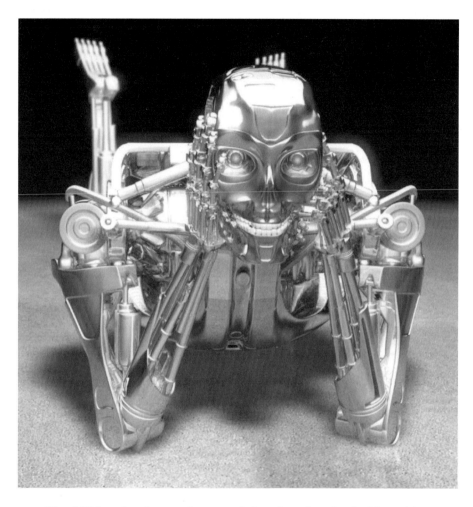

Fig. 4.18 *Imagine the transforms needed to place the robot in this position.*
(Image courtesy James Hans)

In figure 4.17 we see that the geometric data for each element, such as an upper leg or foot, is held as a separate entity, so that it can be modified by specific transform sequences. It also makes modeling easier, for once one leg has been modeled, a second leg can be copied directly, or made from a mirror image of the first leg.

Figure 4.18 shows a robot lying on its front with its chin cupped in its hands. To achieve this pose, a complex sequence of transforms is needed to place each element into its correct position. This would normally take a lot of time, but a good CAS will permit the animator to move individual elements using a mouse. During this process, the software is implicitly working out the transforms needed to effect the movement.

Metamorphosis

We have just seen how hierarchical animation enables objects to be animated over a series of keyframes, and we have also seen, in the previous chapter, how objects can be modeled from a collection of CVs. As CVs are nothing more than numbers, there is no reason why they should not be altered over time. And when they are altered, it gives rise to objects that change their geometric form, which is called *metamorphosis*, or *morphing*.

The method used is to describe the object at appropriate keyframes, with an animation curve to describe the blending process. Each object description must have the same number of CVs. For example, figure 4.19 shows three profile curves formed by their respective CVs, which are used to create surfaces of revolution. If these are associated with three keyframes, it is possible to inbetween them, and automatically construct an object at each frame. As the CVs are in different positions for each frame, the object appears to undergo a metamorphosis. Figure 4.19 also shows the resulting silhouettes of the surfaces of revolution at the three keyframes.

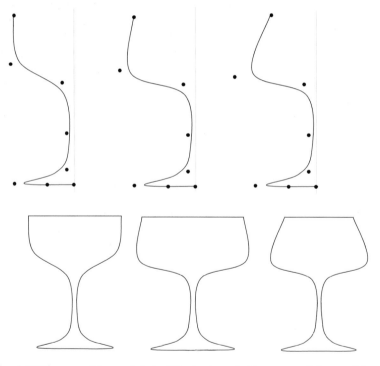

Fig. 4.19 Three profiles and their CVs (top), and silhouettes of the resulting surfaces of revolution (bottom).

Procedural animation

Long before the arrival of commercial animation systems, languages such as FORTRAN and ALGOL were used to produce computer animation. Today, C and C++ have replaced these early languages, although FORTRAN still has a significant following in certain scientific sectors. As GUIs had not yet been invented, animators had to rely upon a library of programs that could be referenced to solve a particular animation problem. The library was continuously extended by new procedures as they were invented. This type of computer animation was known as *procedural animation* as it relied upon explicit programming procedures to move objects, apply textures, adjust lights and render images.

With the arrival of GUIs and commercial animation systems, many procedural tasks could be performed without programming, but even today, procedural techniques play an important role in computer animation.

Most animation systems provide animators with a scripting language that allows animation to be controlled by logical and mathematical expressions. As a simple example, consider the problem of moving an automobile from one position on a road to another. This could be set up using two keyframes with the car positioned at the start and end locations. But say we wanted the car's wheels to turn realistically as it was animated between the two keyframes. To do this correctly we must ensure that the wheels rotate at a speed based upon the distance moved, which means that we must know the diameter of the wheels, and the distance traveled for each frame. Obviously, we could work this out on a calculator and compute the angular rotation for the wheels. But say we altered the position of the keyframes, the key positions of the automobile, or even the diameter of the wheels. We would have to recalculate the angular rotations every time we made such a change. By using the "expression's" feature of an animation system, we can program the computer to undertake this task for us.

To illustrate this, consider the situation shown in figure 4.20. On the left we see a wheel of diameter D located at a starting position A (x_a, y_a, z_a), and on the right, its final position B (x_b, y_b, z_b). The distance between A and B is called *Distance*, which can be calculated using the theorem of Pythagoras. We know that the circumference of a circle is $\pi \times D$; the wheel rotates *Distance* divided by the wheel's circumference $\pi \times D$. Say, for

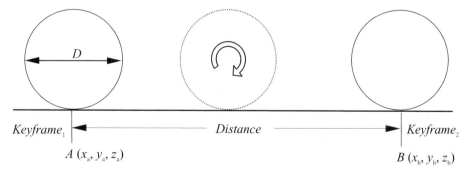

Fig. 4.20 *Computing how many times a wheel rotates over a given distance.*

example, this came to 10 revolutions. It would mean that between *Keyframe*₁ and *Keyframe*₂ the wheel would have to be rotated 3600°. Dividing this by the number of frames gives the angular rotation per frame. This calculation can be embedded as an expression inside an animation system, and no matter how we change the values of *D*, *A*, *B*, *Keyframe*₁ or *Keyframe*₂, the wheel will always rotate realistically. Now this may have seemed a little complicated for those unfamiliar with mathematics, but when scripting is mastered, some very powerful animations are possible.

Forward kinematics

When an animator animates a character using keyframes or with frame-by-frame increments, the final position of the character is determined by the sum of the movements given to the character for each frame. The character's speed, orientation and position are determined by the skill of the animator to get the character into a position by a particular frame. If the action doesn't fit the available time span, the animator has to try again, until it does fit. This process is called *forward kinematics*, as the motion (kinematics) of the animation progresses forward in time.

Inverse kinematics

As human beings, we find it relatively easy to stretch out and pick up a cup, stand on a chair to reach a shelf, or bend down to pick up a box. When undertaking such tasks, we don't have to worry about the joint angles to use between various bones, or even think about maintaining balance — automatic background processes take over, whilst we concentrate on other things. It would be useful if some of these skills could be used in animating a virtual human character. And there is no reason why, one day, such characters should not be endowed with sight, so that they could be programmed to undertake complex tasks such as climbing a ladder, playing a piano or dancing. For the moment, though, these scenarios are still research projects, but the next best thing is called *inverse kinematics*.

Inverse kinematics (IK) is concerned with moving a skeleton from one pose to another. The skeleton is constructed from a hierarchy of bones and joints, much like a human skeleton. But rather than animate every bone and joint with transforms to produce some new pose, key parts of the skeleton are positioned in the required final position, while the computer calculates the transforms for the rest of the skeleton. For example, in figure 4.21 we see a simple skeletal structure in a rest and an an outstretched pose. In order to animate the structure between the two poses, we would normally have to use forward kinematics to obtain new values for the joint angles α, β, θ and then use keyframe animation. The IK technique is much simpler. We simply drag the end of the skeletal arm, the *End Effector*, to the required position in space, and the IK algorithms automatically compute the joint angles to support the pose. The original and final poses can be stored as a keyframes and inbetweened over any number of frames.

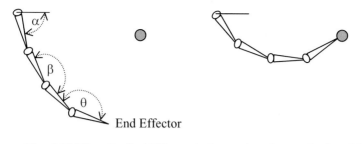

End Effector

Fig. 4.21 *When the End Effector is dragged to the required position,
IK algorithms compute the joint angles.*

Commercial animation systems provide various IK tools for the animator, and it is not worth elaborating upon this technique because a specific IK system will have to be used to illustrate the process. Nevertheless, it is worth pointing out that IK is extremely useful, but it can not solve everything for the animator. For as one might have guessed, there can be an infinite number of ways of positioning a skeleton when an end effector is moved to a new position. Which means that the animator has to constrain the joint angles to enable the IK tools to generate a stable solution.

Another problem for IK is when joint angles have too much freedom. For example, consider the problem of sitting in a chair and reaching out to touch a table. We could constrain our body from moving and attempt to reach the table by arm movements alone. Another approach is to rotate our shoulders to move our arm closer to the table, and another solution is found. Other solutions arise if we allow unusual shoulder rotations. So although IK is very useful, it should not be regarded as the ultimate solution to an animator's problems.

Very often, a character is animated by a mixture of inverse kinematics and forward kinematics. The benefits of IK can be used to ensure that feet remained on the ground during a walk cycle, whilst forward kinematics is used to swing arms and body in an unconstrained manner. But IK will be useful for reaching, or whenever a hand or foot attaches itself to something.

Particle systems

We know that a 3D point with its xyz coordinates is the basic building element in computer graphics, and the three numbers are easily modified using a variety of techniques. For example, we can use the equations that describe the path of a projectile leaving a cannon to determine the coordinate values of a 3D point. And if we displayed the path of this point it would trace out a familiar parabola as shown in figure 4.22.

If we call this point a *particle*, we can construct a collection of particles with random trajectories, speeds, start times, life-spans, etc. These numeric particles are brought to life by placing an object at their coordinate value. The simplest object is a point, which could have position, color and transparency. A GUI for a *particle system* will then permit the animator to locate the source of particles anywhere in space, and associate any object with the particles. Particles are ideal for creating jets of water, smoke, mist,

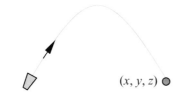

Fig. 4.22 *The projectile traces out a parabolic path due to gravity.*

sea spray, etc., and most systems have presets for hair, fur, stubble, bubbles, candle flame, steam, clouds and cigarette smoke.

If the particles collide with another object they can be programmed to bounce off and continue their brief journey. At the point of collision they could even form the source of new particles and create spray-like effects. Naturally, all of this requires valuable processing time to compute, especially when dealing with tens of thousands of particles. This type of physical simulation is the subject of the next section.

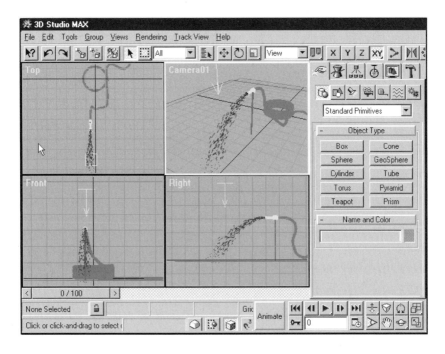

Fig. 4.23 *Setting up a particle source in 3D Studio MAX.*
(Image courtesy DigitalX)

If we start off with a stream of particles that just have random velocities and life times, they will look like a jet of water leaving a hose, but their trajectories will be straight, and not very realistic. To increase the realism we have to introduce some of the natural phenomena, such as gravity, as shown in figure 4.23 and rendered in figure 4.24. But it is very easy to introduce some wind and turbulence, which have a mathematical description. In 3D Studio MAX, the GUI allows the force of the wind to be adjusted interactively until a desired offset is achieved. A final shot is shown in figure 4.25.

Plate 1: "James Bond"
Based upon the drawings of Jean Mulatier
(Image courtesy Chris Tucker)

Plate 2: "Bogie"
Based upon the drawings of Jean Mulatier
(Image courtesy Chris Tucker)

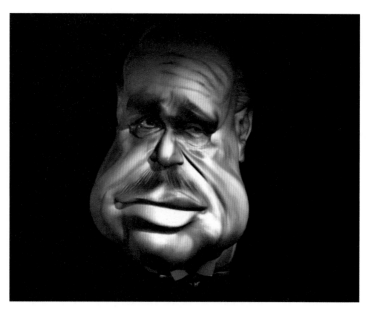

Plate 3: "Marlon Brando"
Based upon the drawings of Jean Mulatier
(Image courtesy Chris Tucker)

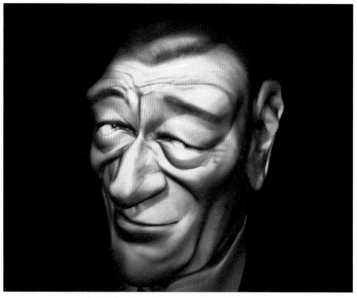

Plate 4: "John Wayne"
Based upon the drawings of Jean Mulatier
(Image courtesy Chris Tucker)

Plate 5: Blue screen shot

Plate 6: Composite image

Plate 7: Compositing images.
(Image courtesy Digital Fusion)

Plate 8: Compositing images.
(Image courtesy Digital Fusion)

Plate 9: Paintbrush character.
(Image courtesy Neil Glasbey)

Plate 10: Insect characters.
(Image courtesy Neil Glasbey)

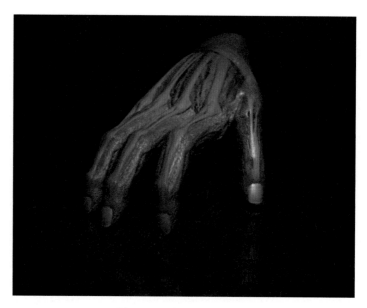

Plate 11: Disfigured hand.
(Image courtesy Nigel Sumner)

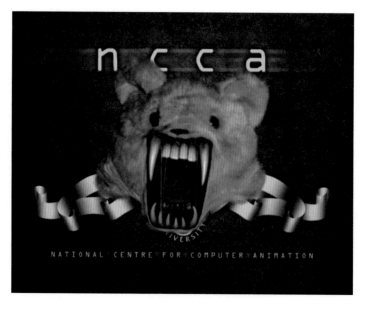

Plate 12: Compositing mouth with bear.
(Image courtesy Nigel Sumner)

Plate 13: Bald and furry.
(Image courtesy James Hans)

Plate 14: Bald and very furry.
(Image courtesy James Hans)

Plate 15: Robot reading a book.
(Image courtesy James Hans)

Fig. 4.24 *Particle water subject to gravity.*
(Image courtesy DigitalX)

Fig. 4.25 *Particle water subject to gravity and wind.*
(Image courtesy DigitalX)

In fact, there are mathematical ways to simulate all sorts of phenomena: magnetic, electrical and gravitational fields, wind, friction, waves and even collisions can be described using equations. This means that once a set of particles is set in motion they can be subjected to these forces to create highly realistic animation. And although mathematics is used behind the scenes to undertake the physical simulation, the animator only has to select the appropriate values in the GUI.

Using simple equations to animate particles is bound to result in predictable movements. However, this can be easily disguised by introducing *turbulence*.

Turbulence is a mechanism for introducing random behavior into animation, and is achieved by modulating coordinates with random values called *noise*. Once more, the animator can control the turbulence parameters through a GUI.

In general, a source of particles can be positioned anywhere in space, and attached to any object — so if the object moves, the particles move with it. Then with the aid of a GUI the animator can control parameters such as the spray direction, angular cone of spray, velocity range, color range, etc., together with the magnitude of gravity, wind and turbulence.

Physical simulation

We have just seen how particle systems can be used to mimic the behavior of certain types of physical phenomena, but various laws of physics can also be used to simulate other behaviors. Physical simulation, as the name suggests, is about simulating physical behaviors within the virtual world of computer animation. Unfortunately, such laws are expressed in the language of mathematics, and at the beginning of this book I promised not to introduce any equations. Nevertheless, I will try to give you some idea how such effects work.

Over the centuries various scientists have discovered relationships between the parameters associated with objects. These include the following:

- The relationship between sides of a right-angle triangle. [Pythagoras]
- How planets move around the sun. [Kepler]
- How objects fall under gravity. [Galileo]
- Calculating gravitational forces. [Newton]
- Describing electromagnetic fields. [Clerk-Maxwell]
- The polarization of light. [Brewster]
- How light moves through a lens. [Boys]
- How light interacts with matte surfaces. [Lambert]

Many of the laws discovered by these people have found their way into computer animation programs. For example, Pythagoras' law about "the square of the hypotenuse equals the sum of the squares of the other two sides" is central to everything that goes on inside a computer animation program. The lens equation discovered by Boys is used in ray tracing to simulate the refraction (bending) of light through a glass lens. And Lambert's law describes how the brightness of a matte surface depends upon the position of the light source, but is independent of the position of the observer. There are hundreds of such laws, and once one understands the underlying mathematics, and can solve these within a computer, they can be used for physical simulation.

Perhaps one of the most useful branches of physics to computer animation is particle mechanics. Here we discover the laws describing the behavior of springs [Hooke's law]; how objects suffer drag when moving through a liquid or gas [Stokes' law], and the laws of motion [Newton]. Such laws can be used to simulate how a heavy object would behave if it were attached to a spring, and allowed to oscillate up and down. The equations would be given the starting conditions such as the spring's stiffness, the mass of the object, and the force of gravity. They would then be solved for different positions in time. At each time step, the position of the object would emerge and be used to control the position of the animated object. If this computation can be undertaken in real time, the animation will appear immediately in front of the animator. If the calculations are so intense that several seconds are needed to solve each time step, the individual frames can be stored on disk and played back in real time after the simulation.

We could also simulate a heavy ball rolling across a floor, hitting a wall and bouncing off, and finally coming to rest. To do this the computer software has to be given parameters such as the ball's radius, its mass, its starting velocity, the position of the wall, and the coefficients of friction. Without friction, the ball would continue rolling forever!

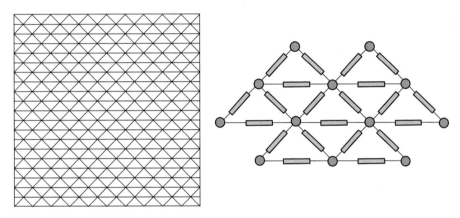

Fig. 4.26 *A triangular 3D mesh representing a piece of cloth (left) and the system of masses and springs simulating the behavior of the cloth (right).*

Another very exciting area of physical simulation is the simulation of cloth. This is achieved by forming a piece of cloth from a 3D triangular mesh as shown in figure 4.26. At the simulation level, each triangle is replaced by three small masses connected by thin springs. If one of the masses is moved slightly, the simulation software computes how forces are propagated throughout the mesh of springs to reach a state of equilibrium. At this point, the positions of the simulated masses are transferred to the 3D mesh of triangles, and the process repeated. When this is performed in real time the cloth is animated with life-like behavior.

Collision detection

When two objects attempt to share the same space in the real world various forces come into play, and the objects move away from one another. In the virtual world of computer animation, because space and objects are represented numerically, objects can share the same space, and it is very easy to animate one object passing through

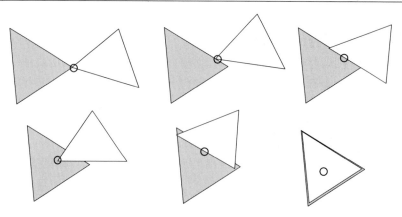

Fig. 4.27 *Six ways a pair of triangles can collide.*

another. If we wish to simulate what happens in the real world, then a strategy is required for *collision detection*.

This is very easy to understand, especially if we consider what happens when two objects built from triangles collide. In fact, all that we need to consider is the interaction between two triangles, as illustrated in figure 4.27. The figure includes the following scenarios:

- vertex to vertex,
- vertex to edge,
- edge to edge,
- vertex to surface,
- edge to surface,
- surface to surface.

And as a vertex, edge and surface have a numerical representation, geometric techniques are available to detect these collision conditions.

When animating within a physically simulated environment and collision detection is activated, all sorts of things become possible. Cloth can be draped over objects, a ball can bounce down a flight of steps, clothes move automatically when a character's limbs move, particles bounce off surfaces, and leaves can fall from a tree without intersecting branches and be blown randomly by a turbulent wind!

To illustrate how computer animation is evolving, consider the simulated image in figure 4.28. A mesh of triangles is used to represent a tray of liquid, which is then disturbed by some moving objects. Automatically, waves propagate across the surface and collide with the objects. The animation continues over a period of time to show how reflected waves interfere with one another. It is a beautiful process and one that I believe will play an increasing role in generating digital content. However, there are problems, in that it is difficult to program the simulation to behave in a particular way. But I am convinced that this will be solved one day. For further details of this software take a look at www.realflow.com.

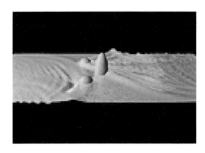

Fig. 4.28 *A simulated water scene.*
(Image courtesy Next Limit)

Rotoscoping

Over the relatively short history of computer animation there has been a great deal of research interest in providing a physical basis to animated behavior, whether it be in the way characters walk, the way objects collide with other objects, or the way a tree sways in the wind. In traditional animation, the most accurate way of animating real-world behavior is through *rotoscoping*. This consists of recording on film the desired movement, and tracing this onto paper or cel. It's a laborious process, but one that works.

Rotoscoping is even used in computer animation. For instance, take the case of animating a 'blob' of milk, with arms and legs that has to walk about on a tabletop. As this is has no physical equivalent, it can be extremely difficult for a computer animator to bring the character to life. A traditional animator is very familiar with animating such organic silhouettes, and can provide the computer animator with a series of frames that can be scanned into the animation software. They are then used by the computer animator as a reference to tweak the computerized 'blob' of milk into similar positions.

Constraints

Animated walk cycles are notoriously difficult to get right, and a classic trick is to keep a character's feet out of view from the camera! The main problem is preventing the character's foot from sliding when it initially touches the floor. With *constraint* software it can be prevented quite easily.

Constraints are concerned with forcing a behavior upon an object, and include things such as constraining a foot to the floor at particular frames. Forcing an object, such as a hand, to touch another object as it is moved about. Or constraining the gaze of a character to follow a moving object.

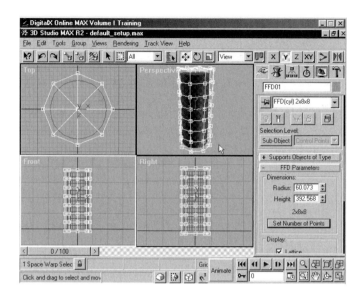

Fig. 4.29 *A cylinder with FFD CVs.*
(Image courtesy DigitalX)

Free-form deformation

Free-form deformation (FFD) is a very powerful technique for modifying the geometry of the whole, or part of an object. To begin with, the animator surrounds the object with an array of CVs as shown in figure 4.29 where we see a cylinder surrounded by a regular lattice of CVs as used in 3D Studio MAX. The animator then has access to various GUI tools to move the CVs to new positions as seen in figure 4.30. Figure 4.31 shows the final rendered object in the form of a bottle.

FFD systems provide commands to bend one end of the box, whilst keeping the other end stationary. Those triangles located where the box bends most become deformed, and those within a volume remaining straight are simply translated to a new position.

Skeletons

Humans, animals and fish have evolved with internal bony skeletons that provide support, protection and mobility. The human skeleton allows us to maintain an upright posture. The spine, with its flexible bone segments, allows us to move the torso and head into various positions, whilst our arms provide support for our hands. The rib cage provides protection for the lungs and heart and the skull protects our brains from external knocks. Joints at the ankles, knees, hips, neck, shoulders, and elbows allow us to walk, run, jump, sit, swim, etc.

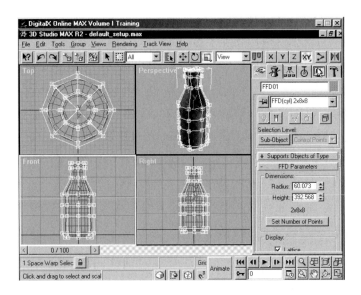

Fig. 4.30 *Modifying the CVs to form a bottle.*
(Image courtesy DigitalX)

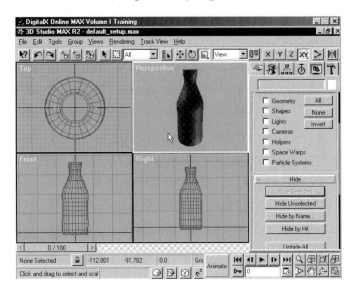

Fig. 4.31 *The final rendered bottle.*
(Image courtesy DigitalX)

As skeletons play such an important role in human and animal articulation, it seems natural that they could play a similar role in animating computer-generated characters. We will examine how a skeleton can be used to move the geometric skin of a character.

To understand the process, let us see how a series of points can be animated to move away from an object. Figure 4.32a shows a series of points and a probe. To animate the points we could program the computer to work out the distance of each point from the probe's tip and move them according to some rule. The rule will ensure that close points will move further than distant points. Figure 4.32b shows the result.

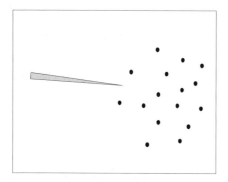
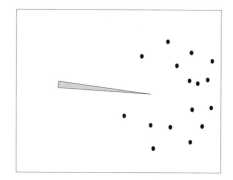

Fig. 4.32a *Probe and some points.*   **Fig. 4.32b** *Moved probe and points.*

Now, say that these points were the vertices of triangles, or the CVs of a network of surface patches. By moving the probe we move the surface. Points close to the probe move much more than distant ones. This is the idea behind using skeletons to animate a character.

We start by modeling a character's surface skin from polygons or patches and use the *skeleton* feature of the animation system. This allows us to construct a jointed skeleton with its bones in the center of its body. If we select a particular bone and move it with the mouse, all the vertices or CVs close to this bone will move according to some proximity rule.

To illustrate this further, consider the situation shown in figure 4.33. On the left we see a cylindrical mesh containing two bones of a skeleton. On the right the bottom bone has been rotated 90° taking with it the associated skin. Notice how the skin is creased on the inside of the elbow joint. In this case the compression is acceptable, but with the wrong rules one could find the skin creasing and intersecting.

The skeleton feature allows the animator to modify the rules to obtain a desired effect. It will also give the animator control over the influence different bones have upon the character's skin.

Another use of skeletons is to use the relative angles of two bones to influence the size or position of an object. For example, figure 4.34 shows a leg containing the animating skeleton. When the foot bone is rotated, the angle between it and the lower leg is used to enlarge the calf muscle. As this enlarges, it pushes against the skin to simulate what happens in reality.

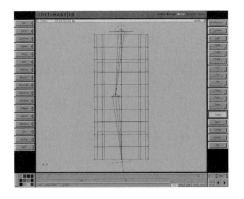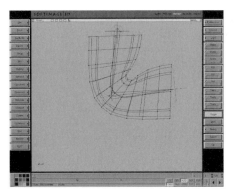

Fig. 4.33 *The image on the left shows two bones of a skeleton in a relaxed state. The image on the right shows how the skin is moved by moving the skeleton. (Image courtesy Neil Glasbey)*

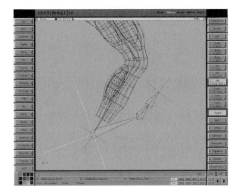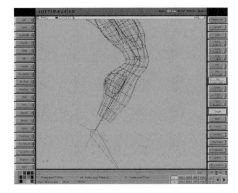

Fig. 4.34 *The image on the left shows a skeleton of bones inside a leg. When the foot bone is rotated, the relative angle between it and the lower leg is computed to enlarge the leg muscles. (Image courtesy Neil Glasbey)*

Conclusion

We have only managed to examine some of the features included in a modern computer animation system. Hopefully, it has given you an insight into what can be done with very little effort.

One of the obvious trends is to let software perform many of the tedious tasks associated with animation, but also undertake some tasks that depended upon the drawing skills of traditional animators. Personally, I believe that this is the right way forward, as it enables us to animate much more complex scenarios and get on with telling the story. For example, if a story calls for a thousand ants to march along a road and one was faced with the choice of animating every individual ant, or using a procedure to perform the work, I know which technique I would use.

But how will this ever end? Who knows, but research in virtual reality is already investigating ways of associating "intelligent" behavior with *vactors* (virtual actors). Perhaps one day, there will be animation systems where characters can be told to enter stage left, walk across the room and shake hands with someone standing by the fireplace. Scripting such a scene seems very difficult, but by then we may even be talking to our computers!

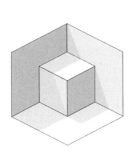

5

Computer Animation Hardware

Introduction

In this chapter I want to describe the hardware used in computer animation. Such hardware is evolving very fast, and rather than concentrate upon specific manufacturer's models, I will describe generic devices and their operational characteristics and refer to specific systems where appropriate. Those readers who wish to discover the technical details of commercially available systems can look at manufacturers' Web sites listed in Appendix A.

Before we start though, it will be useful to explain some of the techniques behind the display technology.

Refresh rate

Refresh rate defines how often the display screen is refreshed with an image — which may be the same image, or a new image. In television technology an image is composed of two parts called *fields*: one field consists of the odd rasters and the other field consists of the even rasters. This is called *interlacing*. Figure 5.1 shows the two fields formed by a television cathode ray tube (CRT). The solid horizontal line is the raster where the image is being refreshed, and the diagonal dashed line represents the fly-back part where the beam is blanked and repositioned for the next raster. Interlacing the odd field followed by the even field keeps the image refreshed. For video technology there is a field and frame refresh rate and table 5.1 shows these speeds for the UK's PAL coding system and the USA's NTSC coding system.

The reason for dividing an image into two parts is to minimize the frequency bandwidth of the broadcast signal, and to reduce flicker by maximizing the refresh rate.

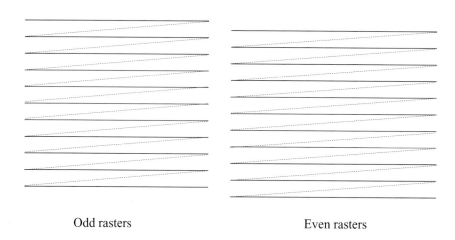

Odd rasters   Even rasters

Fig. 5.1 *The two fields that make a video frame.*

A television receives its new images from the signals detected by its aerial, and as there are a specified number of fields transmitted, all the television circuitry has to do is keep everything synchronized. However, a computer monitor has its image maintained from a portion of memory that is updated whenever the computer is instructed.

Today, most computer monitors are non-interlaced, and the entire frame is refreshed at a speed that causes minimum flicker, and is in the order of 72 Hz.

Table 5.1 *Field and frame rates for the USA and UK.*

	USA (NTSC)	UK (PAL)
Field rate	60 Hz	50 Hz
Frame rate	30 Hz	25 Hz

Update rate

The update rate is the rate at which the *content* of the image is updated. For example, in television, a video camera samples a scene at the video rates shown in table 5.1, which means that the update rate equals the refresh rate. But in a computer, the update rate is determined by the speed at which software is executed. For example, if a computer can only execute the renderer program at 10 Hz, there will only be 10 different images seen every second, but the monitor will still attempt to refresh the screen at its refresh rate. If it takes exactly 0.5 seconds to render an image, and the refresh rate is 72 Hz, the monitor will display the first image 36 times and the second image 36 times.

Computers

Computers come in all shapes and sizes: from the humble PC to the massively parallel supercomputer used for simulating global weather patterns, or cosmological 'big bangs'. Today, however, virtually all computers are able to create pictures of some sort, and are therefore potential candidates as a computer animation platform. But, every computer has processing limitations, which ultimately dictates the complexity of 3D images it can manipulate. We will now take a brief look at PCs, graphics workstations and supercomputers.

PC

We have seen in previous chapters that computer animation software is very complex, and demands ever increasing levels of computational power. A few years ago, there was no chance that a PC could have been used to undertake serious animation projects — however today, the story is completely different.

Most PCs are equipped with some sort of graphics facility to support multimedia applications and the display of 2D and 3D graphics. Although such PCs can display simple graphics, high-performance graphics boards are required to provide the performance needed to support realistic rendering times. Graphics boards will include some of the following characteristics:

- range of resolutions
- large on-board texture memory
- perspective correct texture mapping
- sub-pixel and sub-texel positioning
- texture morphing
- Gouraud modulated textures
- video texture mapping
- anti-aliasing
- number of textured triangles rendered per second
- sustained pixel fill rate
- NTSC/PAL standards
- per-pixel fog, smoke and haze effects

The resolution for monitors is typically $1280(h) \times 1024(v)$ and most graphics boards can cope with this resolution. But because the on-board texture memory is currently around 4MB or more, the range of displayed colors is dependent upon resolution. For example, the Obsidian range of boards display 256, 65K and 16.7 million colors at a resolution of 640×480; but only 256 colors at 1280×1024.

Rendering speeds are measured in terms of how many pixels can be written per second or millions of textured triangles per second, with most boards currently exceeding a fill rate of 100 mega-pixels per second and exceeding 5 million triangles per second. However, one must be careful when comparing board specifications, as triangles are measured in different ways.

Currently, there is a strong movement towards Windows NT PCs, and as the processor clock speed of such machines exceeds 500 MHz, it is inevitable they will become a major force in future computer animation systems. The advantage of these systems is that the PC still remains a PC, and can be used for all of the normal functions of word processing, spreadsheets, slide presentations, etc., as well as supporting computer animation.

One problem that everyone faces when purchasing a computer, especially a graphics computer, is its speed relative to other machines. One cannot go by the processor's clock speed, as this says nothing about the internal architecture, data bandwidths, buffers, etc.

A PC also comes with more than one processor, which means that it can execute two parts of a program in parallel. Software can only take advantage of this feature if it has been designed with a *multi-threading* facility.

Graphics workstation

Computer graphics workstations have always played an important role in supporting computer animation. Their cost varies considerably and they have always outperformed PCs, but today's Windows NT PCs offer comparable performance at a reduced cost, and are vigorously challenging this position.

Computer graphics workstations operate with a UNIX or LINUX operating system, and although they may work with processor clock speeds that are comparable with PCs, it is their internal data channels and architecture that provides the added performance. The UNIX and LINUX operating systems provides an ideal environment for developing software, and given the choice, programmers will always opt for a workstation rather than a PC to develop code.

Graphics workstations are also specified in terms of the rendering speed, and although they provide extra performance, it is not inevitable that this will always be the case. Considerable effort is currently going into the design of more powerful 3D graphics boards, and as their market share increases, the distinction between PCs and workstations is becoming increasingly blurred.

Supercomputer

Certain types of supercomputers generally manufactured by Silicon Graphics, Inc. are often used for high-end computer animation applications. Such machines are used because of the superior rendering speeds, often measured in tens of millions of triangles per second.

Motion capture

In recent years many technologies have emerged to capture the motion of humans. Some of this technology is used in computer animation and some for VR systems. In computer animation, character animation is particularly difficult, especially when a high level of realism is required, and although scripting and keyframe animation can obtain good results, motion capture is often better. However, it introduces its own set of problems, and overall, animators have to rely upon a mixture of techniques to solve their problems.

The technologies currently available include mechanical, optical, ultrasonic and magnetic, and Appendix C lists some popular systems.

Latency and the update rate are two important parameters associated with trackers, and of the two it is the latter that is most important when real-time work is involved. The update rate determines the time taken between measuring a position and its availability to the host software.

Mechanical

A simple mechanical tracker can take the form of mechanical arm jointed at the shoulder, elbow and wrist. When one end is fixed, the 3D position of the other end is readily calculated by measuring the joint angles using suitable transducers. The electro-mechanical nature of the device gives it high accuracy and low latency, but its active volume is restricted.

Optical

One popular form of motion capture employs infrared video cameras that record the movement of a person. Attached to the person is a collection of markers in the form of small balls fixed to critical joints. When the moving person is illuminated with infrared light the marker balls are readily detected within the video images. As the system depends upon line of sight, the orientation of the cameras must be such as to ensure that the markers are always visible. The positions of the markers within the video images are identified by host software, and triangulated to compute their 3D position in space. If the 3D points are stored as a file they can be used at some later date to animate the joints of a computer-animated character to great effect. If, however, the 3D points are input to a real-time computer system they can be used to control some virtual character.

One popular motion capture system is the ExpertVision HiRES system by Motion Analysis Corporation. It supports up to 125 markers and up to 10 cameras, with frame rates from 60 to 240 fps. The system can cope with spins and flips, and compensates for blocked markers by using spline curves and redundant markers.

In Japan, the ExpertVision system has been used to animate the virtual singer *Kyoko*. Kyoko is the brainchild of HoriPro, a Japanese talent agency, and has been modeled from 40,000 polygons with incredible detail. The virtual singer is expected to have a long and commercial career if she can be exported around the world.

The other system from Motion Analysis is their FaceTracker. This captures facial expressions by monitoring the motion of small markers attached to the user's face. As the user's head is also tracked, the data can be used to control the dynamics of an online virtual head. Anticipated markets for this technology are in computer animation, film special effects, 3D Web sites, real-time cartoons, etc.

Electromagnetic

Electromagnetic tracking technology is very popular and is generally used in VR systems to monitor the position and orientation of the user's head and hand. The system employs a device called a *source* that emits an electromagnetic field and a *sensor* that detects the radiated field. The source, which may be no bigger than a 2 inch cube, can be placed on a table or fixed to a ceiling. The sensors are even smaller and are readily attached to the user's body.

When the sensor is moved about in space it detects magnetic fields that encode its position and orientation. The latency of these systems is very low — often less than 10 ms — but another parameter to watch when working in real time is the update rate, as this determines the number of samples returned to the host computer.

Because electromagnetic fields are used, there are no line of sight restrictions, however the active volume is restricted to a few cubic meters, and large metallic objects readily disturb the fields.

Polhemus market a variety of products such as STAR*TRAK, ULTRATRAK, FASTRAK (Fig. 5.2), ISOTRAK and INSIDETRAK. The 3SPACE FASTRAK accepts four receivers for each transmitter, with a total of 8 transmitters (32 receivers) and is widely used for VR and computer animation applications. Its accuracy is 0.03 inches RMS, a resolution of 0.0002 in./in. and a latency of 4 ms. Its standard working range is just over 3 m but can be extended to 10 m with an optional LONG RANDER transmitter.

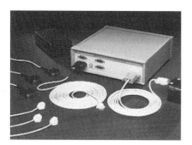

Fig. 5.2 *The Polhemus Fastrak tracker (Image courtesy Polhemus)*

Conclusion

Computer hardware is changing so rapidly that it is pointless including too many technical specifications in a book. Hopefully, some of the concepts described above will help the reader appreciate what to look for when choosing hardware.

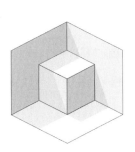

6

Computer Animation Software

Introduction

One of the problems of writing about software is that whilst one is describing the various features currently available, the software company is announcing a new name for the product and is busy developing the next release with a new range of features. So by the time the book is published it is describing products that are totally out of date — which is of little use to the reader.

But I thought that I should say something about software so that you had some idea what was included. And perhaps the best way is to approach the topic at a generic level.

A generic computer animation system

Today, you can choose to run an animation system on a UNIX or LINUX workstation, an NT PC, or an Apple MAC. But not every software product is available on these platforms, therefore before buying a computer, make sure that it supports your preferred animation system.

Today's animation systems include products such as Maya, Sumatra, Houdini, 3D Studio MAX, and Lightwave. They vary in price as well as features, and a safe way to decide which one to buy is to speak to animators who really understand how they work. Don't be surprised to discover that opinions vary greatly. One animator will rave about the modeling feature of one system, but prefer the renderer of another. Someone else will praise the character animation virtues of one product, but prefer the physical simulation features of another. So finding the 'best' system is a futile exercise.

Some of the areas you need to investigate are listed below:

- overall user interface
- ease with which you can move from modeling, to animating and rendering
- ease of modeling
- ease of using NURBS
- procedural modeling tools
- the way particles are incorporated
- image quality of the renderer
- library of texture maps
- ray tracing and radiosity
- selective rendering
- different resolutions
- anti-aliasing
- bump mapping
- quality of shadows
- creating mattes
- animation editor
- keyframing tools
- ease of building skeletons
- interface for inverse kinematics
- physical simulation
- collision detection
- range of shaders
- range of plug-ins
- working with different file formats
- scripting facility
- expressions interface
- help facility
- technical support

Conclusion

Although it can take a long time to understand an animation system, they are reasonably similar and it should not take too long to learn another system. Nevertheless, it is almost impossible to be an expert in more than one system. So it is worth taking some time thinking about the system you are going to adopt.

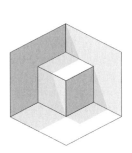

7
Post-Production Techniques

Introduction

Post-production techniques embrace a wide variety of procedures for manipulating images. This can range from a simple change in image brightness to the integration of computer-generated animation with a live action sequence.

As this is a very large topic, this chapter can only make a superficial survey of some of the techniques used in the video and film industries. Furthermore, a computer animator may not have direct control over the post-production process as this impinges upon the role of digital compositors and technical directors. Nevertheless, it is still worth knowing something about what is involved. Consequently, this chapter reviews the nature of a digital image, explores simple image manipulations, and explains how a composite image can be created from two or more elements. To begin with, let us remind ourselves of the nature of a digital image.

Digital images

Spatial resolution

We have seen that a renderer creates an image in the form of a matrix of pixels. The *spatial resolution* (i.e. the number of horizontal and vertical pixels) is determined by the output medium, whether it is paper, television or film. The resolution for television is determined by international standards specified by the NTSC, PAL, SECAM and HDTV systems. However, the resolution for paper and film are application dependent, as much depends upon the paper size and the film format. In film, for example, anything from several hundred to four thousand rasters may be used for a 35mm format, and this could easily increase by 50% for the 65mm IMAX format.

Pixel resolution

Each pixel holds three primary color components: red, green and blue. In general, each color intensity is stored within one byte of memory. These layers of bytes are often referred to as the *red, green* and *blue channels.* You will recall from Chapter 2 that a byte is capable of storing 256 binary combinations, which means that each primary color can have 256 intensities. Binary 0 represents zero intensity and binary 255 represents maximum intensity. Note that the highest intensity is 255 rather than 256, because zero is one of the binary combinations. The total number of colors that can be stored is found by multiplying 256×256×256, which exceeds 16 million hues.

Having 3 bytes for each pixel gives us 24 bits of *color resolution.* If 6 bits were available for each primary color, only 64 primary color intensities would be possible, which would lead to *banding* in the image, where one color intensity changes to another. Unfortunately for us, the human visual system is very efficient at detecting this phenomenon, which is called *Mach banding* after the scientist Ernst Mach.

Some digital systems increase the color resolution to 10 bits. This gives 1024 primary color intensities and provides a total color palette in excess of one billion hues! Whether we can perceive them is another matter. However, this ensures that color banding is completely eliminated, but it does consume more disk space to store the image.

Depth channel

When a renderer computes the primary color values for a pixel it can also compute the depth of the colored surface from the virtual camera. This can be associated with the pixel as a depth value to form the *depth channel.* If one byte is used to store this depth it means that 256 depth values are possible, which is rather coarse. If four bytes are allocated per pixel, there are 256×256×256×256 depth values, which provides for very fine spatial *depth resolution.*

Recent laser-ranging technology makes it possible to calculate the depth of features in real scenes on a pixel-by-pixel basis, which means that it is possible to integrate a computer-generated object with a real scene using their depth channels. This enables a computer-generated object to be moved about a live action scene, and be automatically masked by features in the scene. The depth channel is only used when there is a specific need for the data, otherwise it is omitted to avoid consuming disk space.

Alpha channel

When a transparent feature, such as a window, is rendered, the renderer must be able to compute how much background color is seen through the window. To make this calculation the window must have a transparency property associated with it, normally with a value between 0 and 1. After the calculation, the renderer leaves this transparency value in one byte associated with the pixel. This provides for 256 levels of transparency and forms what is called the *alpha channel.* The alpha channel is a normal feature of any digital image, which now consists of three layers of primary color data, and one layer of transparency data.

Normalized values

Rather than referring to the binary values of a color channel, we can scale the binary range of 0 to 255 between 0 and 1, such that 128 becomes 0.5, for example. Such a process is called *normalizing*.

Color manipulation

Once an image is stored digitally (i.e. as numbers) it is possible to perform all sorts of numerical operations upon the numbers. We could, for example, take the square root of an image! This would involve taking the square root of every primary color value. i.e. a binary color value of 0 (normalized value) would remain at 0 and a binary color value of 1 remains at 1. However, a value of 0.36 changes to 0.6; and 0.64 changes to 0.8, etc. The overall effect brightens the mid-range tones of the image.

Taking the square root of an image is not very useful, but it does illustrate how numbers can be modified by software. In general, images can be added, subtracted and multiplied together. For example, if the color values of two images were added together, the resulting image would contain both images, and appear overlaid, just like a double exposure in a film camera. There is a good chance that the summed color values could exceed the maximum normalized value of 1. But as 1 is the highest normalized value, the final color values have to be clipped at 1.

Similarly, we could multiply the color values of an image by 1.2, say. This would brighten the image slightly, and we could also run into the same problem of intensity clipping. However, if an image were to be multiplied by values ranging between 0 and 1, there is no problem.

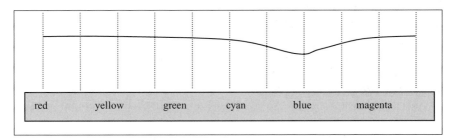

Fig. 7.1 A simple GUI to control color balance in an image.

Color balance

A useful way of modifying the color values of an image is found in a number of digital compositing systems. The color space is displayed as a horizontal window, where colors are depicted as a continuous rainbow of hues. The user then creates a horizontal curve using interactive GUI tools, the shape of which determines the new color balance. Figure 7.1 shows such an arrangement with a curve indicating that certain parts of the blue spectrum are to be attenuated. Peaks in the curve represent color additions, whilst troughs represent color subtractions. The technique is very intuitive as the modified image can be displayed and viewed in real time.

Let us now consider what happens when two images are multiplied together.

Multiplying images

Let's store one image as conventional rgb values as shown in figure 7.2, and the second image as a pattern of black and white pixels in an alpha channel, where black pixels are represented by 0 and white pixels by 255. Their normalized values are 0 and 1 respectively. Let the alpha channel image be such that it consists of a central white square on a black background as shown in figure 7.3.

Fig. 7.2 A reference rgb image.

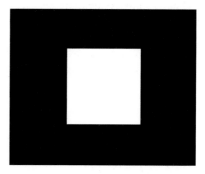

Fig. 7.3 The alpha channel, where white equals 1 and black equals 0.

Fig. 7.4 The result of multiplying the reference image by the alpha channel.

If we now multiply the corresponding pixels of the reference rgb image by the alpha channel, we produce a central square of color image on a black background as shown in figure 7.4. The black background border appears because the associated pixels are multiplied by the alpha channel zeros. And the central square image appears because the associated pixels are multiplied by the alpha channel's 1s. The image stored in the alpha channel is called a *matte,* and is fundamental to compositing.

Mattes

In the above example the matte was very simple and had to be created by someone. It is very easy to imagine the effect of changing the shape of the matte, and even including a gray edge, rather than a sharp transition from black to white. When a gray edged matte is used, the multiplication creates a soft edge to the central square image.

Difference matting

Difference matting creates a matte by subtracting one image from another. For example, say we have two images of the same scene but one of them contains a foreground object. If we subtract the former from the latter the resulting image contains the foreground shape on a black background. The three images in figure 7.5

illustrate how this subtraction process works. Figure 7.5a shows the scene without the foreground element and figure 7.5b is the same scene with the foreground element. If the corresponding pixel values of figure 7.5a are subtracted from figure 7.5b, the resulting matte is created as shown in figure 7.5c. Note that the background is black, but the foreground element still contains detail. The black background in the matte now provides a reference to extract the foreground element from Fig. 7.5b.

Although this sounds like an excellent idea, in practice it is virtually impossible to guarantee that the two images share an identical background. The camera could move slightly between taking the two images, or even the lighting conditions could vary. Thus when the subtraction is made, pixel values will not reduce to zero. Nevertheless, the technique exists and is used, given the right conditions.

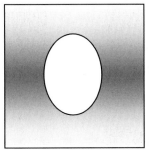

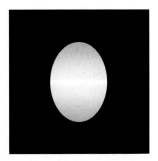

Fig. 7.5a *Background detail.*

Fig. 7.5b *Background detail with foreground element.*

Fig. 7.5c *The result of subtracting the image in Fig. 7.5a from Fig. 7.5b.*

Image compositing

Mattes can also be used to extract a foreground feature of one image composited with a background image, but to do this we need an automatic way of defining the matte's shape.

To simplify the process it is conventional to photograph the foreground image against a blue background. When the foreground image is revealed against a blue background, the blue becomes a natural *key* to unlock the foreground detail from the image. In fact, using blue to create a matte, or any other color, such as green, is called *chroma-keying*.

Inside a computer, software readily isolates the foreground from the background and can output mattes associated with any aspect of the image.

Chroma-keying

The *chroma-key* technique examines every pixel of the foreground image and, where a blue pixel is found, the alpha channel is set to 0. Non-blue pixels have their corresponding alpha value set to 1. The alpha channel now stores a matte defining the shape of the foreground image.

We now require an automatic process to composite the foreground image with the background image. To do this let us introduce some simple notation to describe the compositing process for one pixel. The letters C, F and B identify the corresponding pixel in the composite, foreground and background images whilst the letter M identifies the corresponding pixel of the matte in the alpha channel. The letters C, F and B are subscripted with 'rgb' to remind us that they represent the three primary color components: red, green and blue. And M is subscripted with 'a' to remind us that its value is in the alpha channel. Thus we have:

C_{rgb} = a composite rgb pixel,
F_{rgb} = a foreground rgb pixel,
B_{rgb} = a background rgb pixel, and
M_{a} = an alpha channel matte pixel value (0 to 1)

If the alpha channel stores the foreground matte, the composite image is obtained by the following process:

$$C_{rgb} = M_{a} \times F_{rgb} + (1 - M_{a}) \times B_{rgb}$$

If the alpha channel pixel M_{a} equals 0, the process becomes:

$$C_{rgb} = 0 \times F_{rgb} + (1 - 0) \times B_{rgb}$$

which means that $C_{rgb} = B_{rgb}$. i.e. the composite pixel is set to the background pixel.
If the alpha channel pixel M_{a} equals 1, the process becomes:

$$C_{rgb} = 1 \times F_{rgb} + (1 - 1) \times B_{rgb}$$

which means that $C_{rgb} = F_{rgb}$. i.e. the composite pixel is set to the foreground pixel.
If the alpha channel pixel M_{a} equals an intermediate value of 0.5, for example, the process becomes:

$$C_{rgb} = 0.5 \times F_{rgb} + (1 - 0.5) \times B_{rgb}$$

which means that $C_{rgb} = 0.5 \times F_{rgb} + 0.5 \times B_{rgb}$. i.e. the composite pixel is a 50–50 blend of the two pixels. Table 7.1 summarizes these actions.

Table 7.1 *Summarizes how the composite image is constructed from the foreground and background images.*

M_{a}	$M_{a} \times F_{rgb}$	$(1 - M_{a}) \times B_{rgb}$	C_{rgb}
0.0	0.0	B_{rgb}	B_{rgb}
0.5	$0.5 \times F_{rgb}$	$0.5 \times B_{rgb}$	$0.5 \times F_{rgb} + 0.5 \times B_{rgb}$
1.0	F_{rgb}	0.0	F_{rgb}

The above algorithm is widely used in computer animation to blend one number into another, and is nothing more than linear interpolation.

Blemished mattes

There are a number of problems with chroma-keying that I conveniently ignored, and the first concerns the use of a blue screen. It is possible that the screen contains blemishes or is lit unevenly. This means that the matte in the alpha channel will not be completely black. Some pixels will have non-zero values, which will interfere with the compositing process. To overcome this problem, compositing software packages provide automatic tools for cleaning up blemished mattes.

Color spill

When someone stands in front of a blue screen it is highly likely that some blue light will reflect onto his or her back and be visible around his or her silhouette. This is called *color spill,* and is particularly noticeable in the person's hair. Unfortunately, when such a foreground image is chroma-keyed away from a blue background, the image is contaminated with patches of blue. Fortunately, modern compositing software is very adept at removing these artifacts.

Tracking

The digital nature of computer images permits all sorts of image manipulation and analysis. For example, image-based speed detectors can photograph an automobile moving along a highway, identify the position of the registration plate, and extract its registration code. This is transmitted to the next radar position, which performs the same process. When a registration plate match occurs, the average speed is computed, and a fine levied against any speed offenders. Although we are not interested in estimating the speed of features in a sequence of images, we are often interested in *tracking* the path of a feature over a series of frames.

For example, say we have stored in a computer a short video sequence of a walking man, and we wish to track the path of his nose over the sequence. For each frame we want to compute the horizontal and vertical position of the pixel at the end of his nose. Obviously, we could do this by hand, but compositing software can perform this automatically using a feature recognition algorithm. At the end of the analysis – which may only take a few seconds – the path of the man's nose is known as a sequence of pixel addresses. Say, now, that we wanted to make his nose glow red over the animation. We could paint a small glow icon with a semi-transparent matte. A compositing software package could then be used to move the glow automatically along the path traced by the man's nose and composite the two images. If, when animated, the glow is too bright or too large, the process is quickly repeated with different parameters.

Rendering and compositing

I have probably given the impression that the rendered image is the final image. This may be true in some projects, but in commercial practice, especially where computer elements are integrated with video, it is normal to render different elements separately, so that they can be manipulated individually at the compositing stage. For example, say a teapot is to be animated moving across a tea table, and a shadow is used to integrate it with the scene. If the teapot was rendered together with its shadow and an appropriate matte, it could be that the shadow is discovered to be too light or dark when composited. A quick fix is to render everything again and repeat the compositing process. However, if the teapot and its shadow are rendered separately with their individual mattes, the compositor can manipulate the individual elements to obtain an optimum mix.

Interactive and batch processing

Some compositing exercises may be small enough for a compositor to work interactively at a workstation. However, where long sequences and multiple layers are involved, the compositing exercise is prepared as a batch process and performed in the background or executed overnight. The batch-processing mode is particularly useful when different options need to be explored by a client. For example, a client may wish to explore the effect of changing the brightness of a background. This is readily set up by the compositor, who will script the compositing to be repeated with the different backgrounds.

Plates 7 and 8 show screen shots of the Digital Fusion compositing system. The top right-hand images show the foreground element against a blue screen and the top left-hand images show the composited effect. The bottom left-hand corner contains the GUI used to describe the compositing process.

Conclusion

Compositing is a central feature to computer-generated imagery and very sophisticated software and hardware systems have evolved to support it. Compositing saves time and introduces greater flexibility when different elements have to be integrated. In general, the post-production process requires the animator to output ambient features, highlights, transparency and shadows, with their corresponding mattes, so that the compositor can integrate them correctly with live images. Which is why a good compositor is worth his or her salt, and frequently commands a very high salary.

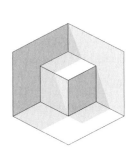

8

Computer Animation Applications

Introduction

Now that we have discovered the techniques behind computer animation it is worth looking at how computer animation is used in various sectors. It may even give you some ideas where to seek employment or a career once you have mastered the subject.

Television graphics

One of the roles of a television graphic designer is to create animated graphics for program titles, news programs, seasonal promotions, current affairs and incidental animations. Prior to computers, live action, scale models, character generators, cel animation and pieces of card would have been used to produce these sequences. However, electronic paint systems, digital compositing systems, and 3D-computer animation have become the everyday tools of the graphic designer.

Digital technology has revolutionized television production. The discrete nature of video images enables them to be stored within a computer, which can then manipulate them as through they were a physical surface. These can be rolled up, peeled back, exploded, shown in perspective, illuminated and composited with other synthetic objects. This integration of computer-generated images with digital video effects has provided designers with a potent creative medium, which appears to have no limitations.

Computer animation is a very flexible medium for creating title sequences for television programs, as it in no way restricts the graphic designer in the media he or she can use. The sequence can be prepared entirely using computer animation, or a foreground sequence could be composited with a live-action background. Even live action can be input to an animation sequence in the form of texture maps, mapped onto moving surfaces.

Real-time animation

Many computers are now able to render images in real time, although not with the same quality that one associates with computer-generated films. Nevertheless, they are ideal for news items where a complex sequence of events has to be visualized. For example, animation depicting an airplane accident may have to be prepared in one or two hours before being broadcast live. Access to an extensive 3D database is vital to such productions, and Viewpoint DataLabs' database is an obvious prerequisite. NURBS are often used to depict a desired trajectory, along which an object can be moved.

Real-time computer animation is often used to visualize the results of national election campaigns. And to cope with the real-time broadcasting of images, procedural animation techniques are used to translate the changing numerical status of political parties into corresponding animation. This is a very powerful technique, but often requires many months of programming and testing to ensure that the system will function perfectly on the day.

Computer games

The computer games sector is currently experiencing an extraordinary period of growth, and there are now hundreds of such companies around the world where computer animation systems are used to develop new games. Although the final computer game runs in real time on a PC or games console, a computer animation system is used to create and animate the 3D models. Low-polygon models have to be created, perhaps with various levels of detail, which then have to be textured, illuminated and animated. Special development tool-kits then provide the interface between computer animation system and the games console.

Many computer games begin with a *full-motion video* (FMV) animation that sets the scene for the player. This animation is computer generated and is a perfect opportunity for an animator to show off skills in character animation and special effects.

Motion capture (MoCap) is widely used throughout the industry to capture complex motions such as jumping, falling, wrestling, fighting, etc. But it is still not a perfect technology, and character animation skills are vital to tidy up MoCap files and merge them together.

Commercials

Computer animation has been widely used in advertising for several years. In fact, at one time, it was the major application for computer animation. Today, computer animation is still very popular, but has become so sophisticated that it is not always possible to detect when it is being used. For example, an entire set may be computer generated, and the rendering is so good that nothing betrays its synthetic origin. Cars, televisions, video recorders, kitchen sinks, animals and even people, find their way into commercials, and the general public are oblivious to the fact that they are often computer generated!

Some of the effects are the result of incredible effort, requiring individual frames to be painstakingly modified to ensure that multiple layers of imagery appear completely seamless. And as the companies commissioned to undertake these projects are also involved in film special effects and the making of computer-generated films, they have access to a tremendous range of software and experienced animators.

Multimedia

In the world of CD-ROMs, computer-generated images are an important source of creative material. And as the cost of generating such images falls, through the use of low-cost PCs and animation software, the multimedia market could become an important user of computer animation.

Computer animation is a perfect medium for showing how complex objects are assembled, how they work, and for taking impossible journeys through the human body or the inside of an automobile engine. Computer animation could be used for teaching a wide range of subjects such as mathematics, engineering, physics, biology, science, geography, history, etc., and some companies have already started developing this content. However, technology is moving at such a pace, it is difficult to predict how long the CD-ROM era will last. Real-time computer animation is already with us in the form of computer games, and this technology will provide a much more exciting medium to implement truly interactive content.

Legal

Although the legal market for computer animation is relatively small, it is being used to translate legal evidence into possible graphical scenarios. Evidence from witnesses can be corroborated or otherwise by modeling a 3D environment and evaluating whether it holds up to scrutiny. For example, it would be possible to assess whether a witness could see what they claimed to see, or whether a sequence of events could have really happened.

In important accidents, computer animation is used to clarify how an automobile crashed or an airplane got into difficulties. But in such incidents, the animation is based upon physical simulation software, rather than the skills of an animator.

Computer-aided design

Virtually everything we use today has been designed using computers. Historically, the CAD process was developed to provide designers with an interface to capture linear dimensions and surface geometry. But as computer power has increased and GUI tools developed, designers have been presented with the ultimate design tool. Today, virtually everything from a spoon to an entire airplane can be designed and visualized using a computer. Sophisticated software allows designers powerful surface and solid modeling tools to sculpt the delicate curves of an automobile's body. These virtual automobiles can be visualized in any color combination, and evaluated ergonomically for driver comfort and safety.

Concept automobiles may look good on paper or even on a display screen, but modern animation and compositing techniques enable them to be driven through existing cities, or even through imaginary cities of the future. Computer-generated automobiles can be used to evaluate simulated crashes, and finite element analysis (FEA) techniques used to predict the structural changes in body panels and internal chassis components.

Automobiles are not the only objects to be animated with such realism. Computer animation techniques are being used to visualize airports, shopping centers, space stations, rail projects, tunnels, inter-state highways, etc.

Virtual environments

Virtual reality (VR) (Vince, 1998) technology has been commercially available since 1988, but it took a further decade to develop appropriate software tools that were useful to potential commercial users. Today, the trend is away from the name 'virtual reality' and towards *virtual environments* (VEs). Unfortunately, VR systems became very focused upon head-mounted displays (HMDs), and the importance of a first-person view of a virtual world. A VE system, on the other hand, accepts that the most important feature is the 3D environment, rather than the display technology. A VE system can be used with a HMD, but it can also be used with a traditional display screen, a projector, a panoramic screen, a dome, or a CAVE.

In the world of flight simulation, VEs have been used for many years. Typically, the 3D model depicts a real airport, complete with runway, terminal buildings, ancillary transport vehicles, airplanes and local weather effects. There is little room for computer animation as everything is controlled by procedural techniques and the real-time signals received from the pilot in the simulator cockpit. However, VEs are now being used in large engineering and architectural projects, industrial concept design, television, science, computational neuroscience, molecular modeling, telepresence, training and medicine. In some of these applications the VE is populated with one or more virtual humans (*avatars*), who walk about and interact with the environment. Due to the current restrictions imposed by the real-time hardware, it is difficult to endow these avatars with life-like behavior. But it is only a question of time when we will be faced with the problem of animating such avatars, and using all of the stop-frame animation techniques in a real-time environment.

The Internet

Virtual environments are starting to play an important role in Internet applications. For example, the Internet is increasingly being used as a sales medium, where customers will eventually want to explore everything from a piece of furniture to a new house. They will want to see such objects in appropriate settings, explore different color schemes and see them from different points of view.

Future scenarios anticipate the use of life-like avatars dispensing information, teaching us new languages, helping us with our homework, advising us on medical matters and tax problems, or simply engaging us in conversation.

Simulation

Simulation is a very exciting area for computer animation and uses animation techniques to visualize everything from the growth of cells to the big bang in the creation of the universe. The technique of FEA (finite element analysis) reduces rigid objects to a lattice of triangles, which can then be subjected to forces and animated over a period of time. CFD (computational fluid dynamics) simulates how gases and fluids interact with solid objects so that natural flow patterns and areas of turbulence are identified. At the heart of such simulation techniques are sound, mathematical, physically-based modeling strategies, where mass, energy, inertia, velocity, acceleration, spin, friction, temperature, gravity have a numerical representation.

But what also appears to be happening is that computer animation is slowly embracing simulation techniques to simplify the task of animation. For why should one struggle to animate a swinging rope when it can be animated accurately using physical simulation, and why try to animate waves created by a ship's bow, when it can be physically simulated? The future of computer simulation is very exciting, and already we are seeing these features appear in computer animation systems and as plug-ins.

Digital special effects

The digital special effects industry has turned out to be a prime area for computer graphics and computer animation. Simply by scanning high-resolution film images into a computer, features of the image can be modified or removed and totally new ones introduced. An actor, who perhaps died many years ago, is readily incorporated into a modern feature by cutting him or her from old film stock, and pasting them alongside current film stars. Similarly, shots that include artifacts of modern life such as power pylons, telegraph poles, skyscrapers, etc. are readily removed without anyone the wiser.

In films such as *Jurassic Park*, *Star Wars*, *Titanic*, *Twister* and *The Matrix* the real star has been the special effect, whether it is a dinosaur or a virtual passenger falling from a sinking ship.

Theoretically, there is no limit to what a computer can undertake in the form of a digital special effect. It is possible to create extinct and imaginary creatures; virtual actors; sky and sea states; crowd scenes; science fiction effects such as time warps, parallel universes, traveling faster than light; time machines; pigs that talk; and frightening futuristic wars. The real artistry, however, is integrating synthetic elements into live action without anyone seeing the joins. For example, color balance is critical. The brightness and contrast ratio of synthetic objects must match those found in the background. Perhaps a real object should cast a shadow over a computer-generated object — if it doesn't our visual system is the first to notice. We expect objects to cast shadows on other objects, and we use shading cues to resolve their position and orientation. We also expect the surface light intensity on an object to alter when it approaches another object such as a wall; the objects may even reflect each other's surface color. It is this attention to detail that makes digital special effects successful.

Computer-generated films

Finally we come to computer-generated films such as *Toy Story*, *Antz* and *A Bug's Life*. Those of us who have been associated with computer graphics since the early days have waited a long time for this to happen. But now that it is possible, we are appreciating the importance of the plot rather than the effectiveness of the renderer, or the ability of the animator. Although the choice of animation systems is limited, they are all good, with some costing only a few hundred dollars. Colleges and universities around the world are creating brilliant modelers, artists and animators. So today, the computer-generated film industry has access to incredibly cheap hardware, very powerful software, and a talented labor force. The real problem is content. Where do we find an interesting story that the public will appreciate? And this has nothing to do with computer animation!

Conclusion

Computer animation is approximately forty years old and is rapidly developing into a major discipline. We have seen above that it is being used across a wide range of applications — but this is only the beginning. Perhaps the biggest application for computer animation is still to come. I believe that education and training will be a major use for computer animation. The teaching of mathematics, science, physics, medicine, geography, history, etc. could all be taught using animation. But what would make it really special would be interactivity. The ability to modify parameters and observe a real-time response. Such a revolution is already underway and there is going to be a huge demand for people who understand how to make this happen.

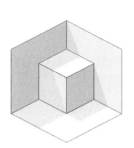

9
Computer Animation Jobs

Introduction

In the traditional sense, animation means bringing drawings to life. For many people, drawing is difficult enough without giving them life-like movements! Consequently, it is understandable why it can take several years to master just some of the basic skills that make a good animator.

Computer animation is not about drawing, but a collection of skills such as modeling, painting and texturing, lighting, camera control, compositing *and* animation. These are all onerous tasks, and rarely do you come across someone who excels in all of them. In fact, in large-scale commercial computer animation productions, it is the norm to have specialists undertake these individual activities. I will describe briefly some of these roles and outline some of the skills expected by various sectors.

Modeler

A modeler creates the 3D geometry for the various characters associated with the project. This process may involve building a physical model that is scanned using a laser digitizer. Special software is then used to bring some sort of order to the unstructured triangles resulting from the scanning operation. Perhaps some of the scanned data will simply provide the modeler with 'keys' to locate surface patches. On the other hand, a character may be created entirely using interactive techniques. There are no hard and fast rules.

A character may consist of several layers of geometry. A horror film, for example, may call for a human skeleton partially covered with flesh and muscles, which are exposed through patches of skin. This zombie might also be partially covered with two or three layers of clothes. Somehow, the modeler must design these layers so that they can be animated individually and integrated without giving rise to geometry clashes. By this, I mean those parts of the zombie's skeleton muscle, flesh, skin and clothing – must not accidentally interpenetrate. It would destroy the whole illusion if parts of the skeleton occasionally appeared through its clothing when animated. Collision avoidance software can resolve such issues but rendering times can escalate to several hours per frame even when using very powerful computers.

The modeler will also incorporate a skeletal structure that will enable the animator to select different parts of the structure and animate them accordingly. To do this, the modeler must have a good idea of how the animator works, and large animation projects require regular discussions between modeler and animator to resolve such problems.

Modelers must also construct the props such as guns, cars, tables, chairs, etc., used by the different characters. These may be designed from scratch, or be available from some in-house database. 3D sets also have to be constructed but, as in film making, only those parts that will be visible by the camera have to be constructed.

The computer games industry places some emphasis on a modeler's ability to construct believable models using the minimum number of polygons. Because a computer game has to run in real time, excess polygons only add to the rendering time. Two further strategies help maintain a game's speed: the first is to employ a variety of characters modeled to different levels of detail. Thus, as the character recedes into the distance, a model with a lower level of detail is substituted. The second strategy is to use rich texture maps to create the impression of fine geometric detail.

Typical skills include:

- drawing
- architecture
- composition
- spatial awareness
- knowledge of mechanical structures
- understanding of anatomy
- knowledge of a computer animation system
- knowledge of computer graphics and computer animation.

Artist

Once the geometry has been defined it is the job of an artist to color and texture the various elements. A range of software tools is available for this process. Photographs can be scanned in from real scenes and surfaces, which are then projected onto various surfaces during the rendering process. Other texture maps may be created using a 2D paint program. One of the problems of projecting a 2D texture onto a 3D surface is the distortion caused by the mapping process. This, however, can be overcome by 3D paint software. Such programs enable an artist to interactively paint detail and texture using the 3D polygonal or surface patch model, to minimize the distortion introduced by projection mapping. If you look carefully at some recent computer-animated films you will notice that some of the characters do undergo visible changes as the story develops. This may be in the form of beard stubble, cuts and marks on clothing, dirt and dust, etc., all of which add to the credibility of the character. This detail has to be prepared by the artist.

The artist is an important person in the computer games industry as painting skills are used to make the low-polygon models look as real as possible. Often, shading and shadows are part of the painted detail, and reduce the amount of work of the real-time renderer.

Typical skills include:

- painting
- drawing
- knowledge of paint programs
- knowledge of a computer animation system
- knowledge of computer graphics and computer animation.

Compositor

In digital special effects, a final shot is often composited from several elements: the set may be a scale physical model shot against a blue screen, which will eventually be replaced by a real sky background. Foreground elements, such as a crowd scene, could be live action shots recorded from an appropriate camera position. Only the main characters may be computer-generated. It is the role of the compositor to integrate these disparate elements into a coherent scene such that the overlays and joins are invisible.

The compositor works with software systems such as Media Illusion and Flame, or hardware systems such as Quantel's Henry. Some of their duties include matte extraction, painting, rotoscoping, color balance, and 2D effects.

Typical skills include:

- UNIX and shell scripting
- knowledge of a computer animation system
- knowledge of a commercial compositing system
- knowledge of computer graphics and computer animation.

Character animator

Traditional animators are familiar with the problems of endowing their line drawings with mass and volume; the human emotions such as pain, joy, anger, laughter, crying; as well as activities such as running, jumping, falling, dancing, lifting, spinning, etc. The role of the computer character animator is to bring a computer character to life with the same, if not more, realism.

Some production companies still believe that the best way of acquiring such skills is to spend some time working in traditional animation, and transfer these skills to the computer domain. Personally, I am not convinced that this is necessary today. There is no doubt that the time would not be wasted for someone who had never studied the mechanics of motion. But I still believe that someone who understands how animals, people and objects move can apply this knowledge to a computer animation system without first learning about 2D animation techniques.

Not everyone is cut out to be a character animator. Some computer animators can animate a rotating logo, a walking robot, or a ship rocking on the sea with ease, but when it comes to animating a running animal or a walking human character, they lack the essential observational skills that distinguish a good character animator from an ordinary computer animator. So don't be disappointed when you discover just how difficult it is to perfect a walk cycle.

Typical skills include:

- drawing
- observational skills
- understanding of anatomy
- knowledge of special effects techniques
- knowledge of human and animal behavior
- knowledge of a computer animation system.

Enveloper

Enveloping is a term used by Industrial Light and Magic (ILM) to describe the animation of skin and muscle attributes of a creature or character. An *enveloper* is a person who extends an animation sequence by adding extra dynamic attributes to a character as it moves. This may be in the form of muscle movement, inertial sways in the body as it walks, or how flesh and bone reacts to gravitational forces as a creature adopts different postures.

Typical skills include:

- modeling
- animation
- observational skills
- understanding of anatomy
- knowledge of UNIX and shell scripting
- technical knowledge of computer graphics
- knowledge of a computer animation system.

Technical director

Technical director (TD) is a top job in film special effects. He or she is responsible for a series of shots associated with a film. They normally have a sound experience of digital special effects, covering all of the job functions described above. Although the job calls for excellent management skills, it also involves real hands on ability to solve and resolve problems encountered by other members of their team.

Typical skills include:

- modeling
- animation
- drawing and painting
- sound practical experience
- UNIX and shell scripting
- knowledge of compositing
- knowledge of computer graphics
- knowledge of one or more computer animation systems
- knowledge of in-house software.

Conclusion

This chapter identifies some of the roles found in computer animation and generally associated with the large production companies. Smaller production houses cannot afford to maintain so many specialists and rely upon multi-talented people who can model, texture, animate, illuminate, composite, and even program their computer when things get tough. Such people do exist, and when one thinks about it, their jobs are much more exciting than someone who performs the same thing day-in, day-out.

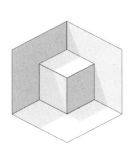

10
Animating

Introduction

We have almost come to end of this journey through the essentials of computer animation and perhaps the reader is thinking that computer animation is not so difficult after all. To a certain extent this is true, and having covered virtually everything from the principles of computer graphics to the career prospects in computer animation, we have overlooked just one thing: How does one learn to animate?

A traditional cartoon animator requires very little technology to create animation — a pencil, eraser, some paper, cel and a camera. However, we must not forget that the animator must be able to draw and bring their drawings to life. This demands tremendous observational skills, a knowledge of anatomy, human psychology, walk cycles, runs, exaggerated actions, humor, timing, composition, editing, etc., etc. None of these have anything to do with the technology of pencil and paper.

A computer animator must possess even more skills, as he or she is working in three dimensions and, in many cases, is faced with simulating photo-realistic images and physically-based animation. They, too, must be able to bring their images to life, and computer technology can be just as passive as a pencil and paper in this respect. A computer animator must still possess tremendous observational skills, knowledge of anatomy, human psychology, etc., etc., and this book will not help you acquire such skills. So before moving to the concluding chapter, let's explore some ideas that are fundamental to successful animation.

Weight, mass and inertia

We all know what we mean by the weight of an object. For example, every morning I stand on my bathroom scales and weigh myself. What I am really doing is finding out how much the Earth is attracting me through the action of gravity. Newton summarized the attractive force between two objects as being proportional to the product of their masses, and inversely proportional to the square of their distance. For example, if the mass of one object is doubled, the attractive force is doubled. But if we keep the masses constant, and double the distance separating them, the force is not halved, but reduced to a quarter of its original value. Furthermore, if I weigh myself on the Moon using my bathroom scales, my weight is greatly reduced. This is because the Moon has less mass than the Earth, and does not attract my body so much. Yet the mass of my body has not changed.

The mass of an object is a measure of its inertia — that is, its resistance to being accelerated by a force – and we still do not know how it arises. The weight of an object changes depending whether it is located on the Earth or the Moon, whereas the mass of an object is constant. However, this is only true for speeds less than approximately 30,000 Km/sec. Einstein proved in his famous $e = mc^2$ equation that as the velocity of an object approaches the speed of light (300,000 Km/sec) its mass increases dramatically, and theoretically becomes infinite at the speed of light.

Newton was not aware of this phenomenon, but he did know that an object would continue in its state of linear motion, unless it was acted upon by some external force. Furthermore, the force needed to change an object's direction was directly proportional to the object's mass.

Weight and mass play an important role in making animation believable. For example, when a character is lifting a heavy box, it has to apply an upward force opposing the force caused by gravity. Even if the box can be lifted, its inertia will prevent it from being moved too fast. Next time you see someone attempting to lift a heavy object, or even if it happens to you, observe what is going on. Think about the forces that are being transmitted through the hands and arms to the shoulders, and the impact this has upon the spine and the legs. Notice that as the box is being lifted how it disturbs the center of gravity of the body, which continuously adjusts its attitude to remain in balance. Note that because of its inertia, the object cannot be moved instantaneously. An appropriate force must be applied to effect the desired acceleration. Also, consider the behavior of a person in a crouching position where a heavy object is being cradled in his or her arms. The object's inertia, together with the reactive movements of the body creative an oscillating motion, and can easily induce instability, and force the person to drop the object or fall over with it.

Weight and mass play an important role in cartoon animation where 5 ton weights drop regularly from the sky squashing characters into pancakes. Other characters swing anchors about with impunity, and then forget to let go, and are taken violently stage left. Sledge hammers and anvils also make wonderful icons to communicate that we are dealing with really massive objects.

Center of gravity

The *center of gravity* of an object is an imaginary point where an object's mass can be considered to be located. For example, the center of gravity for a sphere is located at its center and for a rectangular box it is where two diagonals intersect. The center of gravity for a car is not in the physical center of the car's volume, but approximately just above the floor of the car. This is because most of the car's mass is in its engine, gearbox and transmission, which are generally located low in the car's chassis.

The center of gravity for a pencil is halfway along its length, and in the center of its cross-section. The reason why it is difficult to balance a pencil on one end is because its center of gravity can easily move outside its footprint. Figure 10.1a shows a stable pencil standing on its end and figure 10.1b shows a pencil leaning over a few degrees such that its center of gravity falls outside of its footprint. At this point the pencil is destined to fall over.

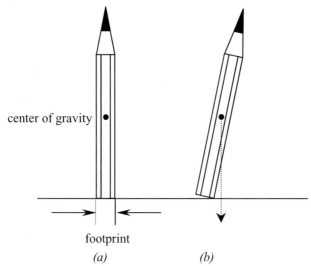

Fig. 10.1 *(a) A stable pencil with its center of gravity located within its footprint. (b) A falling pencil with its center of gravity outside its footprint.*

Being able to imagine where an object's center of gravity is located can help make your animation more realistic. It will help especially in cases where objects fall to the ground and roll about randomly until they find some position of equilibrium. Such falls are very difficult to animate. And our everyday experience of the way things fall, roll, bump and bounce about, makes us very critical when we see computer generated tumbles that look too constrained.

Simulation software can be very effective in animating such sequences, and I see nothing wrong in using this software to solve such problems.

Kinetic energy and momentum

When a force is applied to an object it will accelerate for as long as the force is applied. We know that we must use energy to apply a force, and this energy is imparted to the object in the form of *kinetic energy*. If the moving object is brought to rest by hitting a wall, for example, its kinetic energy will be used to damage the wall, create some noise, generate some heat, or even cause the object to explode into pieces. These pieces will in turn inherit kinetic energy and continue on some sort of journey. The object, or bits of it, eventually comes to rest when all of the kinetic energy is dissipated by being converted to another form.

Everyday experience of the real world has taught us that we should be afraid of cars traveling towards us, as they possess dangerous amounts of *momentum* (mass×velocity), whereas when someone strikes a balloon on our head it can be ignored, because its momentum is insignificant in spite of its high speed.

The idea of momentum is vital in creating realistic animation, as it provides physical cues that we expect when objects interact. For example, when a light plastic ball rolls across the floor, its momentum is small, and its speed is easily reduced by air resistance and imperfections in the floor's surface. Thus when it hits a heavy object such as a chair, its momentum is insufficient to move the chair. The chair's inertia opposes any attempt to move it, and the ball bounces away until it comes to rest. In practice, the ball will apply a small force to the chair and attempt to move it, but frictional forces between the chair and the floor will probably prevent it from moving.

If we repeat the exercise using a heavy marble ball, the result is completely different. The ball will roll majestically towards the chair, and when it collides, it will accelerate the chair. Eventually the chair will stop moving through frictional forces and the ball will be reflected away, and continue rolling until its energy is dissipated.

It is amazing how much information we extract from small visual cues such as a chair moving when hit by a ball. Without being told, we know instantly that the ball was heavy and probably solid. It is this attention to detail that makes good animation.

Bouncing and restitution

When a ball is held at some height above the ground, the Earth is attracting it downward through a gravitational force. The instant it is let go, the ball's acceleration is 9.8 metres per second per second, but its velocity is zero. After one second its acceleration is still 9.8 metres per second per second, but its velocity is now 9.8 metres per second. After two seconds its acceleration is still 9.8 metres per second per second, and its velocity is now 19.6 metres per second. Thus we see that the constant downward gravitational force gradually increases the ball's speed by 9.8 metres per second every second. When an object falls from a very high altitude, air resistance prevents its velocity from increasing beyond a certain point. For example, if you jump from a plane at a high altitude you will accelerate to a speed of about 200 Km/hour. You will then have a little time to glide around until the reducing distance between you and the ground reminds you that pulling the parachute cord is a useful act to dissipate your kinetic energy, and prolong your life!

When a rolling ball hits a wall obliquely it bounces away in a predictable manner. In fact, it behaves like light where the angle of reflection equals the angle of incidence. These angles are shown in figure 1.0.2. The speed of the reflected ball is slightly reduced because when the ball strikes the surface, its kinetic energy is absorbed completely by the surface, reducing the ball's speed to zero. The elastic properties of the surface are such that it will force the ball away and with a fraction of the original energy. This fraction, which is always less than 1, is called *restitution*. The missing energy appears as heat or was used to chip a few molecules away from the surfaces during the impact.

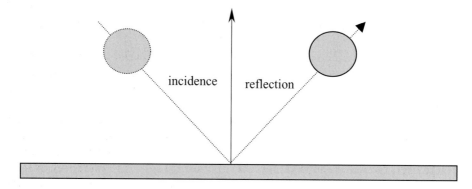

Fig. 10.2 *The angle of reflection equals the angle of incidence.*

Tumbling objects are particularly difficult to animate, especially when they are irregular. The reason for this is that we acquire so much knowledge of the world through unconscious observation that we seem to have an intuitive understanding of how paper behaves in the wind, how a dislodged roof moves in the path of a tornado, or how a house brick behaves when it falls on a pile of similar bricks. When such objects are animated, the slightest deviation from their natural behavior is noticed immediately. A common fault is to constrain their movements with slow speeds and obvious trajectories. This communicates confused characteristics of momentum and inertia. A little chaotic behavior in the form of random spins, changes of direction and jerks normally resolve the situation.

A simple solution to this problem is to use the simulation tools offered by many animation systems. Why not let the computer calculate how a tumbling object should behave? It's very effective, but purists might consider this as cheating. Not at all! We are using computers in the first place to take the tedium from drawing, shading, lighting, working out perspective, moving the camera, etc., so why shouldn't the computer reduce the tedium of physical simulation, so that we can get on with telling a story?

Character animation

Character animation concerns the association of human behavior with an animated character whether it is a human or some creature. Films, such as *Toy Story*, *A Bug's Life* and *Antz*, have taken character animation to incredible limits by bringing toys and insects to life with amazing realism. Facial expressions, hand gestures, body posture, and human characteristics such as eye blinking, nose twitching, scratching, etc. are all included just to add that extra level of realism.

One particular human activity that is difficult to animate is walking, which is often described as a controlled fall. To appreciate this statement, stand up and still. Then slowly start to walk and observe the attitude of your body. You will probably notice that the action begins with a slight leaning forward of the body to disturb its center of gravity. And just like an unstable pencil you start to fall forwards. A natural response is to place a leg forward to control the fall. By the time your foot strikes the floor, your body has gained sufficient energy from falling that this momentum can be directed forwards by repeatedly placing one foot in front of the other. Your momentum is maintained by imparting further forward forces through our leg muscles, and a simple *walk cycle* keeps you moving.

When walking we always have one or both feet on the floor. It is only when we start running that both feet lose contact with the ground. At the turn of the 19th century it was not known how a horse's legs behaved whilst galloping. To resolve the problem a photographer, Eadweard Muybridge, set up a series of cameras to capture the horse's motion. The resulting images showed the horse at different stages of the gallop cycle. He went on to photograph all sorts of human activities that were published in his well-known book *Animals in Locomotion*. These images are often rotoscoped and the coordinates used to animate computer characters.

Muybridge also laid the foundations for the photographic film effect *Time-Slicing*, as used in the film *The Matrix*. For more information on this process, take a look at the web sites listed in Appendix A.

When we start walking, the first couple of steps are small, but we quickly develop a regular pace to keep us in motion. When we want to come to a stop, we anticipate a few steps ahead that our momentum must be lost, and achieve this by reducing the length of our step, and our leg muscles absorb our kinetic energy. We also use the length of our step to turn corners.

Walking, however, is not just a question of moving forward at a constant speed with swinging legs. The body's forward speed is not constant. A gentle pulse modulates it as the feet come in contact with the ground. The pivoting action of the legs forces the body to rise and fall, and sway left to right as each leg performs its task. The hips rock, the arms swing, and neck muscles attempt to keep our head from disturbing our center of gravity.

Computer animators can use a variety of techniques to achieve a walk cycle such as key frames, forward and inverse kinematics, and special features offered by different animation systems. But perhaps the easiest of all is motion capture. One can download MoCap files from the Internet and animate characters with great realism. Is it cheating? Of course not, but MoCap data still presents serious problems for the animator as it is still difficult to 'tweak' the data and integrate different sequences into a continuous animation.

Facial animation

Another major problem for computer animators is facial animation, which can be divided in two: facial expressions and talking. Fred Parke undertook some pioneering research work into animated faces in the early 1970s (Parke, 1972) and in 1988 Keith Waters submitted his Ph.D. thesis *The Computer Synthesis of Expressive 3D Facial Character Animation* (Waters, 1988). They have since collaborated to produce a book *Computer Facial Animation*, which is essential reading for anyone interested in this area.

One of the main problems in facial expressions is constructing a facial model that supports the strong emotions we exhibit through our face such as happiness, anger, fear, surprise, disgust/contempt, and sadness, and the secondary expressions like interest, calm, bitterness, pride, guilty, pain, exhaustion, shame, irony, insecurity and skepticism. This was an area of research investigated by Keith Waters. He found that he could simulate these expressions by creating a polygonal mesh for a face based upon the physical muscle structure of a human. Manipulating the vertices of the mesh could then create a particular expression. This technique enabled a series of expressions to be stored as keyframes, which could be inbetweened to animate the face from one mood to another. This technique is still used today, although NURBS are used as well as polygonal meshes.

One of the most difficult human characteristics to animate is talking. Just the smallest mistake in animation completely destroys the illusion. If the lips are incorrectly formed, or the teeth are not positioned correctly, then it is impossible to associate a voice with the character. In fact, recent research has shown that we do use lip synchronization with someone's voice to interpret what is being said, as well as what is being spoken.

To appreciate the complexity of the problem look at your own face in a mirror when saying some of the following sentences: 'If I', 'If you', 'If we', 'I owe you?, 'We should dance', 'Be careful' and 'Jump now!'. Now there is nothing special about these sentences, apart from the fact that they illustrate the wide range of facial expressions we use when speaking. Even with MoCap data, lip synchronization is difficult, therefore you should not be dismayed if you find this subject difficult to master.

Character animation does not stop at walking and talking. Just consider how you would animate the following emotions and activities:

- crying, laughing, shouting, giggling, snoring, eating, drinking, biting, coughing, blowing, chewing, gargling, singing, sucking, and sneezing
- confusion, exhaustion, pleasure, and pain
- falling, running, jumping, swimming, sitting, standing, hopping, dancing, dressing, swinging, boxing, sweeping, fishing, typing, writing, sword fighting, climbing, sewing, washing, shaving, and diving
- playing a piano, violin, guitar, drums, double bass or trumpet, and conducting.

To conclude this chapter, I would like to draw your attention to some of the images in the color plates section. They are all taken from animation projects undertaken by undergraduate and postgraduate students at the National Centre for Computer Animation at Bournemouth University.

Plates 9 and 10 are taken from a short cartoon by Neil Glasbey. Neil only took one year to master computer animation and discover that he possessed a natural gift for character animation. Plate 10, in particular, illustrates his flair for bringing characters to life.

Plate 11 is taken from an animation by Nigel Sumner who used Maya to animate a realistic disfigured hand. The image reveals the extraordinary attention to detail that Nigel took to model the skeleton, tendons and flesh. Nigel also had some fun compositing the wet mouth and teeth in the toy bear shown in 12. Plates 13 and 14 illustrate Lightwave's fur growing feature. Fur and hair are exciting areas of research and various plug-ins are available for this effect.

Finally, plate 15 depicts the robot modeled by James Hans, reading an early manuscript of this book!

Conclusion

We could go on discussing other problems in animation such as animating spinning objects, swinging objects, cloth, turning the pages of a book, sea spray, spilling liquid, hair blowing in the wind, waves, flying birds and butterflies, etc. etc. But they are extremely difficult and beyond the scope of this book. They are problems you will eventually encounter, and they cannot be resolved by looking up a technique in a book. It is something you have to discover for yourself by trying it out on a computer. It will take time. A very long time, but it will be fun!

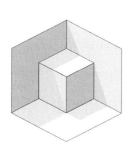

11
Conclusion

There is nothing magic about computer animation. It is based upon sound ideas and techniques that have a geometric and mathematical basis. But this does not prevent someone without such skills from understanding the subject and becoming a brilliant animator.

Having read this book you may be thinking of getting your own computer and animation software. If you do, you will never have a spare moment of time. If you don't, you are missing out on a lot of fun. There is so much to learn and master, and just when you feel that you know a particular animation system backwards, a new version comes out and the process starts again!

Computer animation can be very frustrating, as it is not possible to model and animate everything to the level of realism you may desire and in a realistic time-scale. A computer animation system may not provide you with the tools you need to solve a problem, and you must be prepared to spend endless amounts of time finding a solution. This could require you to learn computer programming, so that you can write a plug-in, which is not so daunting as it sounds.

But at the end of the day, when you have mastered the subject, there is a tremendous satisfaction in admiring a piece of personal animation and saying "I did that, it's all my own work!"

That's all folks!

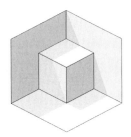 # *Glossary*

Absolute coordinate system   Sometimes used in place of the world coordinate system.

A-buffer   A hidden-surface removal algorithm developed by Loren Carpenter at Lucasfilm as part of the Reyes renderer.

Accommodation   The eye's ability to alter the shape of its lens to focus on objects near and far.

Achromatic light   Light without color.

Acuity   The eye's ability to resolve fine detail.

Acute angle   An angle less than 90°.

Adaptive progressive refinement   A rendering technique used in radiosity that improves the image over a period of time.

Additive color mixing   Creating colors by mixing two or three different colored lights.

Additive primary colors   Red, green and blue.

Aim point   The gaze direction of the observer in world coordinates.

Algorithm   A mathematical or logical procedure for solving a problem in a finite number of steps.

Aliasing

(a) **Spatial**:   Visual artifacts such as jagged edges caused by insufficient spatial sampling.

(b) **Temporal**:   Animation artifacts such as 'wagon wheels' apparently rotating backwards caused by insufficient temporal sampling.

Alpha channel   A video channel derived from the alpha value associated with each pixel in a video frame store, used for storing mattes when compositing images.

Alpha value   See **Alpha channel**.

Ambient light   The background level illumination used by an illumination model.

Ambient reflection coefficient   A fractional value associated with a reflective surface that determines the level of ambient light reflected.

Angle of incidence   The acute angle formed by the surface normal and the incident ray illuminating the surface.

Angle of reflection   The acute angle formed by the surface normal and the reflected ray away from the surface.

Angle of refraction   The acute angle formed by the refracted ray and the reflected surface normal for a transmissive medium.

Angle of view   The solid angle of incident light transmitted by a lens.

Angular velocity   The rotational velocity about an axis.

Animation   The technique of creating moving scenes by projecting a sequence of images in rapid succession.

Anti-aliasing   Strategies for removing or reducing aliasing artifacts arising from insufficient spatial or temporal sampling.

Anti-clockwise polygon   Has its interior to the left when its boundary is traversed in the direction of its edges.

Aperture   A measure of the physical area associated with a lens, through which light can pass.

API see **Application Programming Interface.**

Application Programming Interface (API)   An interface to a software package whereby a programmer can gain access to its internal features.

Approximating spline   A curve that approaches its CVs without intersecting them.

Artifact   Unwanted visual features introduced by a type of technology or an inaccurate algorithm.

Aspect ratio   The ratio of the vertical to horizontal dimensions of an image or shape.

Assembler   A program that converts a simple computer language into binary machine code.

Attributes   Object properties such as color, surface texture and mass.

Average normal vector   A surface normal vector derived by averaging the normal vectors from a group of neighboring polygons.

Axis   (a) A straight line about which operations such as reflection and rotation are performed. (b) A straight line used to construct a system of axes, as in Cartesian notation.

Back clipping plane The rear plane in the viewing pyramid controlling the distance up to which objects are visible.

Back face The unseen side of a polygon.

Back face removal The removal of all back-facing polygons before a scene is rendered.

Bar sheets Used in animation projects as a reference document controlling dialog, music and movements with frame numbers.

Behavioral animation Simulates effects such as flock centering, collision avoidance, and velocity matching.

Bézier curve A curve generated by computing the spatial coordinates of a point on the curve using a series of CVs.

Bézier surface patch A surface patch employing a matrix of CVs to define its geometry.

Binary A number system using a two-state code.

Bit An individual element of a binary-coded item.

Bit map An image formed from digital bits.

Blending function A function used to blend together or interpolate two or more numeric values.

Boundary representation A modeling strategy where objects are represented by a boundary skin.

Bounding box A rectangular bounding volume that completely contains an object.

Bounding sphere A spherical bounding volume that contains an object.

B-rep See **Boundary representation**.

B-spline space curve A smooth parametric curve whose shape is determined by a string of control vertices.

B-spline surface patch A smooth parametric surface patch whose shape is determined by a matrix of control vertices.

Bump map A 2D image for making a surface appear bumpy.

Bump mapping Perturbs a surface normal during rendering to create a bumpy surface.

Byte A group of 8 bits.

C A computer programming language.

C++ An object-oriented version of C.

CAD   Computer Aided Design.

Camera coordinate system   A Cartesian axial system associated with a virtual camera.

Cartesian coordinates   2D or 3D offset measurement relative to some defined origin and system of orthogonal axes.

CAS   Computer Animation System.

Cel animation   Traditional animation that uses thin sheets of celluloid (cel) to hold the images.

Center of projection   The point through which all projection lines pass.

CFF   See **Critical fusion frequency**.

Character animation   A generic term for a animating life-like characters.

Character skinning   The process of defining a surface skin to a 3D character.

Clipping   Removes unwanted objects from a scene.

Clockwise polygon   Has its interior to the right when its boundary is traversed in the direction of its edges.

Collision avoidance   Strategies to prevent virtual objects from colliding.

Collision detection   Strategies to detect collisions between virtual objects.

Color attributes   Color values assigned to an object that enable it to be rendered.

Color bleeding   When the color of one object is reflected in another.

Color model   A color space such as RGB or HSV.

Color space   A 2D or 3D method for organizing colors.

Color table   A look-up table whose entries store color descriptions.

Compiler   A program that converts a high-level computer language into binary machine code.

Compositing   The process of integrating one image with another.

Cone   A receptor in the retina responsible for color vision.

Constraints   Physical limits used to restrict an object's behavior.

Constructive Solid Geometry (CSG)   A modeling strategy for building objects using the Boolean operators: union, subtraction and difference.

CPU   An acronym for Central Processing Unit.

Critical Fusion Frequency (CFF)   The frequency at which a flashing image appears continuous to the eye.

CRT   Cathode Ray Tube, used for television and computer screens.

CSG   See **Constructive Solid Geometry**.

Culling   The action of identifying and removing objects from a view of a scene.

Cyberspace   A popular name given to the virtual domain created by the Internet.

Database   A collection of related records organized such that particular classes of records are easily accessed.

Data structure   A method for organizing data within a computer program.

Degree   A unit of circular measurement. $360°$ = one rotation.

Depth buffer   See **Z-buffer**.

Depth of field   The distance over which an in-focus image is created in a lens.

Diffuse reflection   When a perfect matte surface reflects light equally in all directions.

Diffuse reflection coefficient   A fractional value used to control the amount of diffuse light reflected from a matte surface.

Diffuse surface   A surface that reflects light equally in all directions.

Digitizer   A system for capturing 2D or 3D Cartesian coordinates.

Directional light source   A light source that emits light in only one direction.

Distributed light source   A light source that radiates light over a defined area, rather than from a single point.

Dodecahedron   A platonic object constructed from 12 regular hexagons.

Dynamic constraints   Physical constraints, such as mass and inertia, associated with moving objects.

Easing   The technique of altering the speed of an animated object.

Edge   A line connecting two vertices.

Elastically deformable objects   Objects such as flags, faces, curtains and plastic materials.

Elastic collisions   Associated with colliding rigid objects.

Environment mapping   A rendering technique where background reflections are seen in an object's surface.

Euler's rule   States that, for a polyhedron without holes, the number of edges is two less than the sum of the faces and vertices.

Explicit geometry   Geometry described by numerical values, rather than by algebraic functions.

Explicit surface   A surface defined with explicit geometry.

Extruding   A modeling technique where a 2D cross-section is used to create a 3D volume.

Facet   A planar surface element.

Facet normal   A vector positioned 90° to a facet's surface.

Fairing   See **Easing**.

Far plane   See **Clipping**.

F-curve   A curve describing an animation parameter.

FEA   See **Finite Element Analysis**.

FFD   See **Free-Form Deformation**.

Field   The odd or even lines of a video frame.

Field of view (FOV)   The largest solid angle where incident light can form an image.

File   A collection of related data.

Finite Element Analysis (FEA)   A technique for simulating dynamic stresses in an object.

First degree equation   A linear equation.

Flat shading   A process where a polygon is shaded with a single color.

Flicker   Occurs when an image is not refreshed fast enough.

FMV   See **Full-motion video.**

F-number   The focal length of a lens divided by its 'stopped' aperture.

Focal length   The distance to the focal plane of a lens where an image is in focus when the incident light is from a distant source.

Focal plane   Where a lens forms an in focus image.

Form factor   The fractional radiant energy leaving one patch and arriving at another as used in radiosity.

Forward dynamics   Concerned with computing an object's acceleration when an applied force is known.

Forward kinematics   Refers to the use of transformations in controlling the future position of an object.

FOV   See **Field of view**.

Fovea   The high-resolution central zone of the retina.

Fractal   A data set that exhibits fractal properties as defined by one of a number of dimension rules.

Fractal surface   A surface exhibiting fractal properties.

Frame   Two fields of an interlaced image, or one non-interlaced image.

Frame store   A memory device for storing one video frame.

Free-form deformation (FFD)   A technique for distorting 2D and 3D objects.

Free-form surface   Describes a class of surfaces that have no explicit geometric definition.

Front clipping plane   The near clipping plane representing the minimum distance where points are visible in the viewing pyramid.

Front face   The side of a polygon containing the surface normal.

Full-motion video (FMV)   An animation sequence played at the start of a computer game.

Fusion frequency   The frequency when a flashing image appears continuous to the human visual system.

Gamma   A parameter controlling the light output from a CRT.

Geometry   A description of the shape of an object and its surface characteristics.

Global illumination model   A lighting model that attempts to simulate the phenomena found within complex environments such as multiple reflections, shadow penumbrae, color bleeding, as well as diffuse and specular reflections.

Gloss coefficient   Controls the degree of gloss exhibited by a surface, and is the specular exponent term in Phong shading calculations.

Goal-oriented animation   Techniques used for animating articulated structures subjected to various physical constraints, in which the structure can be given a goal in terms of a final position of one of the elements, and the orientation of the entire structure can be computed.

Gouraud shading   A shading technique that interpolates color over a surface.

Graphical user interface (GUI)   A graphics-based user interface.

Graphic primitive   A shape or object used by a graphic system to construct more complex scenes.

Graphics package   A software system that undertakes a graphics task for a user, such as animation, modeling or painting.

Graphics tablet   A small digitizer frequently associated with a workstation for the input of graphical data, or controlling the screen's cursor.

Graph plotter   A device for creating line-based drawings.

Gray levels   The number of discrete intensity levels of a display device.

Gray-scale image   An image formed from different levels of gray.

GUI   See **Graphical user interface**.

Half space   Two half spaces are created on either side of a planar surface.

Hermite curve   A parametric cubic curve sensitive to the end point tangents.

Hidden-surface removal   A rendering strategy for removing invisible or masked surfaces.

Hierarchy   An organization of things connected in such a way that a unique path exists between any two.

HSV   Hue, Saturation and Value.

HSV color model   Uses the attributes of hue, saturation and value to describe a color.

HTML   An acronym for HyperText Markup Language. A file specification supporting hyperlinks.

Hue   The attribute given to a color that describes its relative position within the visible spectrum.

Hue circle   Colors organized in a circle such that any hue can be specified by an angle between 0° and 360°, or by a fractional number.

Hz   Means cycles/second. Named after the scientist Hertz.

Icon   An image symbolizing an action or thing.

Icosahedron   A platonic object constructed from 20 equilateral triangles.

IG   See **Image generator**.

IK   See **Inverse kinematics**.

Illumination model   A basis for describing the behavior of light with a surface.

Image generator (IG)   A computer capable of rendering images in real time.

Image plane   Synonymous with the picture plane.

Image space   A 2D plane where a projection of a 3D scene is captured.

Implicit surface   A surface with an algebraic description such that its geometry is implicitly defined by coordinates rather than by algebraic functions.

Inbetweening   The process of generating new images from a pair of keyframes.

Incident light   The light that arrives at a surface and is the basis for computing the reflected light received by the virtual camera.

Index of refraction See **Refractive index**.

Instance A reference to a master object.

Instance transform A transformation matrix applied to an instance.

Interactive computer graphics A computer interface that supports real-time, two-way, graphical interaction.

Internet The world-wide network of computers that communicate with each other using a common set of communication protocols known as TCP/IP.

Interpenetrating objects Objects that share a common position in space.

Interpolating spline A curve that intersects its CVs.

Interpolation The process of computing intermediate values between known values.

Interpreter A program that interprets a high-level computer language, one statement at a time without converting it into binary.

Inverse kinematics (IK) A technique for computing how an object should move to arrive at a known position.

I/O An acronym for Input/Output.

Jaggies A popular name for the staircase stepping associated with pixel-based screens.

JPEG A graphics file format developed by the Joint Photographic Experts Group.

Keyframe A specific frame in an animation.

Keyframe animation An automatic process for generating images from a pair of scenes called keyframes.

Knot The join between two curve segments forming a spline; represented by a parametric value.

Lambert's cosine law States that the light reflected from a dull matte surface is proportional to the incident light and the cosine of the angle between the incident light and the surface normal.

Latency The time delay (or lag) between activating a process and its termination.

Level of detail (LOD) The amount of detail or complexity displayed in an object.

Light source A virtual source of illumination used by the renderer to calculate light levels on a surface.

LOD See Level of detail.

Material A definition of the surface characteristics of an object, such as color, shininess, texture and transparency.

MEL Maya's Embedded Language.

MIDI Musical Instrument Digital Interface. A standard for digital music representation.

MoCap See **Motion capture.**

Model A geometric representation of an object produced by a CAD system or 3D modeling package.

Modeling The action of building a virtual object or character.

Momentum The product of mass and velocity.

Monochrome The use of one color as in black and white photography.

Motion capture (MoCap) Capturing the motion of humans using optical or magnetic tracking technology.

Mouse A pointing device used for controlling a screen's cursor.

MPEG A graphics file format developed by the Moving Picture Experts Group.

Multimedia An integrated computer presentation including graphics, audio, text and video.

Network A set of interconnected computers.

Normal vector A vector orthogonal to some surface.

NTSC The National Television Standards Convention is a television standard widely used in the U.S.A.

Object oriented A programming methodology where items of data are described as objects possessing characteristics that can be inherited by other objects.

Object space The coordinate system in which an object is defined.

Octahedron A Platonic object constructed from eight equilateral triangles.

Orthogonal At right angles.

PAL The UK's television standard.

Palette A collection of colors.

Paradigm A pattern or model.

Parameter A quantity that has an effect on a system.

Particle system A collection of discrete particles used to model natural phenomena.

Persistence of vision The eye's ability to record a visual signal after the stimulus has been removed.

Phi phenomenon   How a light source appears to move when one light is switched off, and another, close by, is immediately switched on.

Phong shading   A shading technique that introduces reflective highlights into a surface.

Photorealism   Highly realistic computer-generated scenes.

Photoreceptors   The rods and cones that convert light into nerve signals.

Physical simulation   Algorithms for simulating physical behavior.

Picture plane   A projection plane used to capture an image, especially for perspective projections.

Pitch   The rotational angle about a horizontal x-axis, orthogonal to the forward-facing z-axis.

Pixel   The smallest addressable picture element on a display.

Planar polygon   Has its vertices in one plane.

Plug-in   A program that can be 'plugged into' a larger program to achieve a specific function.

Polygon   A shape bounded by straight edges.

Polygonal mesh   A boundary structure formed from a collection of polygons.

Polyhedron   An object having a polygonal surface.

Polyline   A chain of straight line segments.

Procedural animation   The automatic animation of objects using computer procedures.

Procedural modeling   The automatic modeling of objects using computer procedures.

Procedure   An algorithm.

Properties   The attributes associated with an object such as color, position and behavior.

Radiosity   A global illumination model for computing light intensities resulting from multiple diffuse reflections.

RAM   Random Access Memory.

Raster   One line of a frame or field.

Ray tracing   Uses the geometry of light rays to render a scene.

Real time   An instantaneous reaction to any changes in signals being processed.

Refractive index   A measure of how much light is deviated from its normal straight path, when it passes from one medium to another.

Refresh rate   The frequency at which a raster display refreshes its screen.

Renderer   A program for creating a shaded 3D image.

Rendering   The process of projecting a 3D object onto a 2D display, clipping it to fit the view, removing hidden surfaces and shading the visible ones according to the light sources.

Resolution   A measure of a system's ability to record fine detail.

RGB   Red, Green and Blue. A color space where a color is represented as a combination of the primary colors red, green and blue.

Rigid body   An object whose geometry is fixed.

Rods   Light receptors in the retina that are active in dim lighting conditions.

Roll angle   The angle of rotation about the forward-facing heading vector.

Saturation   The purity of a color in terms of the white light component and the color component.

Scaling matrix   Changes the size of an object relative to some point.

Scanner   An input device for converting photographs into a digital form.

Scripting language   A computer language that is interpreted and executed sequentially, such as MEL.

Second degree equation   A quadratic equation.

Shading   The process of coloring an object.

Skeleton   A skeleton-like structure used to animate a 3D character.

Soft objects   Objects modeled from mathematical equations.

Surface attributes   Qualities such as color and texture.

Surface of revolution   See **Swept surface**.

Surface patch   A surface description that can be used to form a complex surface.

Swept surface   A 3D surface formed by rotating a contour about an axis.

Tetrahedron   A Platonic object constructed from four equilateral triangles.

Texture map   A 2D pattern image for use as surface decoration.

Texture mapping   Substituting detail stored within a texture map onto a surface.

Third degree equation   A cubic equation.

Torque   A force that makes an object rotate.

Tracking   Monitoring an object's 3D position and orientation.

Triangulation   Reducing a shape into a triangular mesh.

Twisted facet   A polygon defined with vertices that do not lie in the same plane.

Update rate   The rate at which a process is modified.

Value   Is equivalent to the term lightness when describing colored light.

VE   See **Virtual environment**.

Vertex   The end of an edge.

Virtual environment (VE)   A 3D data set describing an environment based upon real-world or abstract objects and data.

Virtual reality (VR)   A generic term for systems that create a real-time visual/audio/haptic experience.

VR   See **Virtual reality**.

Winged-edge data structure   A data structure designed to support the geometric integrity of polygons, edges and vertices.

Wire frame   A 3D object where all edges are drawn, producing a 'see through' wire-like image.

World coordinate space   A Cartesian coordinate system used for locating 3D worlds.

World Wide Web   The collection of documents, data and content typically encoded in HTML pages and accessible via the Internet using the HTTP protocol.

Yaw angle   A angle of rotation about a vertical axis.

Z-buffer   A rendering technique for removing hidden surfaces.

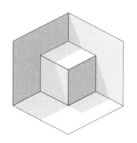

Appendix A
Useful Web Sites

Animation software

Alias|Wavefront
  http://www.aw.sgi.com/

Credo Interactive, Inc.
  http://www.credo-interactive.com/

DreamTeam Ltd.

  http://www.dreamteam-Ltd.com/

Greenworks
  http://www.greenworks.de/

Kadara, Inc.
  http://www.kaydara.com/

ShadowCaster, Inc.
  http://www.shadowcaster.com/

Side Effects
  http://www.sideeffects.com/

Softimage
  http://www.softimage.com/

Softimage knowledge base
  http://vizlab.beckman.uiuc.edu/softimage/kb.html/

Stageware, Inc.
  http://www.stageware.com/

Sven Technologies, Inc.
http://www.sven-tech.com/

Compositing

AVID
http://www.avid.com/

Photron
http://www.photron.com/

Conferences

3D Festival
http://www.3dfestival.com/

ACM Siggraph
http://www.siggraph.org/

EuroGraphics
http://eg99.dsi.unimi.it/

Conversion tools

LambSoft, Inc.
http://www.lambsoft.com/

Okino Computer Garphics, Inc.
http://www.okino.com/

Digitizing hardware

Immersion Corp.
http://www.immerse.com/

Minolta
http://www.minolta.com/japan/rio/vivid/

Paraform, Inc.
http://www.paraform.com/

Real 3D
http://www.real3d.com/

Tricorder Technology plc
http://www.tricorder.co.uk/

Facial animation

Beam, Inc.
http://www.famoustech.com/

Techimage Ltd.
http://www.techimage.co.il/

Magazines

3D Artist Magazine Home Page
http://www.3dartist.com/

Computer Graphics World
http://www.cgw.com/

DV Live Home Page
http://www.dv.com/

PC Magazines
http://www.pcmag.com/

Motion capture

Ascension Technology Corp.
http://www.ascension-tech.com/

Digits 'n Art Software
http://www.DnAsoft.com/

Eptron
http://www.eptron.com/

Motion Analysis Corp.
http://www.motionanalysis.com/

Polhemus, Inc.
http://polhemus.com/

Protozoa, Inc.
http://www.protozoa.com/

Puppet Works
> http://www.puppetworks.com/

SIMI Reality Motion Systems GmbH
> http://www.simi.com/

Vicon Motion Systems
> http://www.vicon.com/

X-IST Realtime Technologies
> http://www.x-ist.de/

Plug-ins

Alias|Wavefront, Inc.
> http://www.aw.sgi.com/plug_ins/

Areté Image Software, Inc.
> http://www.areteis.com/

CIRAD-UNIL
> http://www.cirad.fr/amap/amap.html/

Pixar Animation Studios
> http://www.pixar.com/

Pty Ltd.
> http://www.headus.com.au/

Puffin Designs, Inc.
> http://www.puffindesigns.com/

The Foundry
> http://www.thefoundry.co.uk

Programming

AAF
> http://www.microsoft.com/aaf/

Nate Robins GLUT Home
> http://www.cs.utah.edu/~narobins/glut.html/

OpenGL
> http://www.sgi.com/Technology/OpenGL/

Useful companies

3Dark
> http://www.3dark.com/

3Dcafe
> http://www.3dcafe.com/asp/default.asp/

3D Construction Co.
> http://www.3dconstruction.com/

3DRing
> http://www.3dring.com/

4Division
> http://www.4division.com/

Adobe
> http://www.adobe.com/

Alias Wavefront
> http://www.aw.sgi.com/

Animated People
> http://freespace.virgin.net/animated.people/

Animation World Network
> http://www.awn.com/

Apple Computer
> http://www.apple.com/

AVID
> http://www.avid.com/

Centropolis
> http://www.centropolis.com/portal/

Compaq
> http://www.compaq.com/

Digital Domain
> http://www.d2.com/

Discreet Logic
> http://www.division.com/

Hash
> http://www.hash.com/

Intergraph
> http://www.intergraph.com/

Lightscape
> http://www.lightscape.com/

Lucasarts
http://www.lucasarts.com/

Lucasfilm
httP://www.lucasfilm.com/

Lume
http://www.lume.com/

Lumis
http://www.lumis.com/

MentalRay images
http://www.mentalray.com/

MetaCreations
http://www.metacreations.com/

Microsoft
http://www.microsoft.com/

Newtek
http://www.newtek.com/

Numerical Design Ltd
http://www.ndl.com/

Okino
http://www.okino.com/

PhotoModeler
http://www.photomodeler.com/

Pison
http://www.pison.com/

POV-Ray
http://www.povray.org/

Quantel
http://www.quantel.com/

RealFlow
http://www.realflow.com/

Rhinoceros
http://www.rhino3d.com/

Silicon Graphics
http://www.sgi.com/

Softimage links
http://vizlab.beckman.uiuc.edu/softimage/links.html/

Softimage small reference manual
   http://beauty.gmu.edu/~billv/686/3dimg.html/

Sony
   http://www.sony.com/

Warner Bros
   http://www.warnerbros.com/

Unreal
   http://www.unreal.co.uk/

Unrealed
   http://www.unrealed.net/

Time-Slice Web sites

   http://www.realefex.com/Frames/multicamframe.html
   http://www.whatisthematrix.com/
   http://www.virtualcamera.com/

Other Useful Sites

   http://webreference.com/3d/
   http://www.visualfx.com/
   http://www.vfxhq.com/
   http://www.vfxpro.com/

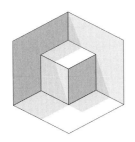

Appendix B
A RenderMan Shader

```
/*
 * glow(): a shader for providing a centered "glow" in a sphere
 */
surface
glow( float attenuation = 2 )
{
        float falloff = I.N;        /*Direct incidence has cosine closer to 1. */

        if (falloff<0) {            /*Back of sphere only */
            /*Normalize falloff by lengths of I and N */
            falloff = falloff * falloff / (I.I * N.N) ;
            falloff = pow(falloff, attenuation);
            Ci = Cs * falloff;
            Oi = falloff;
        } else
            Oi = 0;

}
```

Reproduced from *The RenderMan Companion* by Steve Upstill (Upstill, 1989)

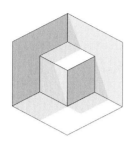

Appendix C
Motion Capture
Hardware

The following table identifies some motion capture systems currently available.

Product	Tech.	Positional Accuracy	Positional Resolution	Angular Accuracy	Angular Resolution
ADL-1	M	0.2"	0.025"		
BOOM	M	0.16"			0.1°
Logitech	A	0.004"	0.004"	0.1°	0.1°
Digisonic	A		<0.005"		0.1°
Ascension	E	0.1°	0.03"	0.5°	0.1° at 12"
Polhemus Isotrak II	E	0.1" at <30"	0.0015"	0.75° at <30"	0.1°
Polhemus Fastrak	E	0.03" at <30"	0.002"	0.15° at <30"	0.05°
UNC	O		<2mm		<2°
ELITE	O	1/24,000 of FOV	1/65,536 of FOV		
Wayfinder-VR	I			±2°	±1°
Vector 2X	I			2°	2°
TCM2	I			±0.5° to ±1.5°	0.1°

Technology key: E = Electromagnetic   I = Inertial
                             M = Mechanical   O = Optical
                             A = Acoustic

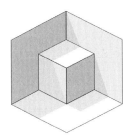

References

Blinn J.F. (1978) Simulation of wrinkled surfaces. *SIGGRAPH 78*, 286—292.

Blinn J.F. and Newell M.E. (1976) Texture and reflection in computer generated images. *CACM*, **19**, 542–547.

Bui-Tuong Phong. (1975) Illumination for computer generated pictures. *CACM*, **18**(6), 311–317.

Catmull E.E. (1974) *A subdivision algorithm for computer display of curved surfaces*. PhD thesis, Department of Computer Science, University of Utah.

Cook R.L. (1984) Shade trees. In H. Christiansen, ed., *Computer Graphics* (SIGGRAPH '84 Proceedings), **18**(3):223—231, July 1984.

Ebert D.S. *et al*. (1998) *Texturing and Modeling*. 2nd Edition. San Diego: Academic Press.

Gouraud H. (1971) *Computer display of curved surfaces*. PhD thesis, Department of Computer Science, University of Utah.

Gregory R.L. (1986) *Eye and Brain: the psychology of seeing*. London: Weidenfeld and Nicolson.

Parke F.I. (1972) Computer generated animated faces. *Proceedings ACM National Conference*, Boston, Vol. 1. 451—457.

Parke F.I. and Waters K. (1998) Computer Facial Animation. AK Peters.

Upstill S. (1989) *The RenderMan Companion*. Reading: Addison-Wesley.

Vince J.A. (1998) *Essential Virtual Reality*. London: Springer-Verlag.

Waters K. (1988) *The Computer Synthesis of Expressive 3D Facial Character Animation*. PhD Thesis. Department of Computer Animation, Middlesex Polytechnic.

Williams L. (1983) Pyramidal parametrics. *SIGGRAPH 83* 1–11.

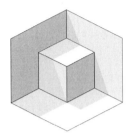

Bibliography

3D Human Modeling and Animation
By Peter Ratner
ISBN: 0-47129-229-X

3D Photorealism Toolkit
John Wiley & Son
ISBN: 0-47125-346-4

Advanced Animation and Rendering Techniques
By Alan Watt and Mark Watt
Addison-Wesley

Albinus on Anatomy: With 80 Original Albinus Plates
By Robert B. Hale and Terrence Coyle
ISBN: 0-48625-836-X

American Cinematographer Manual
Compiled and Edited by Charles G. Clarke
Assisted by Three W. Tyler
An Official Publication of the American Society of Cinematographers

Anatomy Coloring Book
By Wynn Kapit and Lawrence M. Elson
ISBN: 0-06455-016-8

Anatomy for the Artist
By Jeno Barcsay
ISBN: 0-706071-690-0

The Animation Book
By Kit Laybourne
Crown Publishers/Three Rivers Press

Animation from Script to Screen
By Shamus Culhane
St. Martins Press

The Animator's Handbook
By Tony White
Phaidon

The Art and Science of Digital Compositing
By Ron Brinkmann
Morgan Kaufmann

Artistic Anatomy
By Paul Richer
Watson-Guptill

Cartoon Animation
By Preston Blair
Walter Foster

Character Animation in Depth
By Doug Kelly
The Coriolis Group
ISBN: 1-56604-771-4

Chuck Amuck
By Chuck Jones
Avon Books
ISBN: 1-56010-084-2

Cinematographer's Field Guide
KODAK Motion Picture Camera Films

Color Atlas of Anatomy: A Photographic Study of the Human Body
By Johannes W. Rohen *et al.*
ISBN: 0-68330-492-5

Compositing Pictures
By W. Donald Graham
Van Nostrand Reinhold

The Computer Image
By Alan Watt and Fabio Policarpo
Addison-Wesley

Creating 3D Animation – The Aardman Book of Filmmaking
By Peter Lord and Brian Sibley
Harry N Abrams
ISBN: 0-81091-996-6

Creating Special Effects for TV and Film
By Bernard Wikie
London: Focal Press
New York: Hastings House

Digital Character Animation2
By George Maestri
New Riders
ISBN: 1-56205-930-0

Facial Expression
By Gary Faigin
Watson-Guptill
ISBN: 0-82301-268-5

Industrial Light + Magic
By Thomas G. Smith
New York: Ballantine Books

Industrial Light + Magic: Into the Digital Realm
By Mark Cotta Vaz & Patricia Rose Duignam
New York: Ballantine Books

The Illusion of Life: Disney Animation
By Frank Thomas and Ollie Johnston
Hyperion
ISBN: 0-7868-607-0

Inside Softimage 3D
By Anthony Rossano
New Riders Publishing
ISBN: 1-56205-885-1

Melloni's Student Atlas of Human Anatomy
By June L. Melloni (Editor), *et al.*
ISBN: 1-85070-770-7

Professional 16/35mm Camerman's Handbook
By Verne & Sylvia Carlson
American Photographic Book Publishing Co., Inc.

Special Effects in Motion Pictures
By Frank P. Clark
Society of Motion Picture and Television Engineers, Inc.

Special Optical Effects in Film
By Zorian Perisic
London: Focal Press

The Technique of Special Effects Cinematography
By Raymond Fielding
Communication Arts Books
Hastings House

The Technique of Special Effects in Television
By Bernard Wikie
London: Focal Press
New York: Hastings House

Timing for Animation
By Harold Whitaker and John Halas
London: Focal Press
ISBN: 0-24051-310-X

Index